TEACHERS AS MENTORS

TEACHERS AS MENTORS

Models for Promoting Achievement With Disadvantaged and Underrepresented Students by Creating Community

Aram Ayalon

Foreword by Deborah W. Meier

1996–2011   15TH ANNIVERSARY

Stylus
PUBLISHING, LLC.

STERLING, VIRGINIA

KH

Sty/us

Cover: Top photograph courtesy of Fenway High School. Bottom photograph by Ido Cohen.

Published by Stylus Publishing, LLC
22883 Quicksilver Drive
Sterling, Virginia 20166-2102

Library of Congress Cataloging-in-Publication-Data
Ayalon, Aram, 1954-
  Teachers as mentors : models for promoting achievement with disadvantaged and underrepresented students by creating community / Aram Ayalon.—1st ed.
    p.   cm.
  Includes bibliographical references and index.
  ISBN 978-1-57922-310-6 (cloth : alk. paper)
  ISBN 978-1-57922-311-3 (pbk. : alk. paper)
  ISBN 978-1-57922-607-7 (library networkable e-edition)
  ISBN 978-1-57922-608-4 (consumer e-edition)
  1. Teenagers with social disabilities—Education (Secondary)—United States—Case studies.   2. Mentoring in education—United States—Case studies.   3. Mentoring in education—Israel—Case studies._ I. Title.
  LC4092.A93 2011
  373.18269'4—dc22

                                                     2010046669

13-digit ISBN: 978-1-57922-310-6 (cloth)
13-digit ISBN: 978-1-57922-311-3 (paper)
13-digit ISBN: 978-1-57922-607-7 (library networkable e-edition)
13-digit ISBN: 978-1-57922-608-4 (consumer e-edition)

Printed in the United States of America

All first editions printed on acid free paper that meets the American National Standards Institute Z39-48 Standard.

Bulk Purchases

Quantity discounts are available for use in workshops and for staff development.
Call 1-800-232-0223

First Edition, 2011

10 9 8 7 6 5 4 3 2 1

7/18/12

To my wife, Michal Ayalon Bouhadana,
who is my mentor

CONTENTS

ACKNOWLEDGMENTS

First and foremost I would like to thank the students and staff as well as parents at both Kedma School and Fenway High School. They were generous in opening themselves to me and sharing their experiences, hopes, and aspirations.

More specifically, I would like to thank Kedma's current principal, Michal Hadad, as well as the former principal, Moshe Shriki, and the first and founding principal, Clara Yona-Meshumar. All three were willing to dedicate time to me despite their busy and demanding schedules. In addition, I would like to thank the head of the "Friends of Kedma" organization—Ilana Yona, who provided me with invaluable information. I would also like to thank mentors who took me under their wings and provided me with special attention and help and who became my friends over the years, including Yardena Chemo, Ezra Avnaim, Rafi Gur, Shlomit Deri, Ilanit Alphi, Yael Kalil, Yaniv Danino, Yiska Hazan, Margalit Levitan, and Hagit Cohen Eliahu. Special thanks also to secretary Hani Halik and assistant principal Miri Cohen.

At Fenway High School, I would like to thank the current principal, Peggy Kemp; the assistant principal, Kevin Brill; and the former principal and founder, Larry Myatt. In addition, warm thanks to the advisors: Keith Hammitt, Eileen Shakespear, Rawchayl Sahadeo, Elisa Van Voorhis, Chadwick Johnson, Anthony Rhodes, and Brian Gonsalves.

This book would not have been possible without financial and sabbatical support from Central Connecticut State University and more specifically the School of Education and Professional Studies, headed by dean Mitchell Sakofs. I would also like to thank my publisher and editor John von Knorring of Stylus Publishing for his dedication, thoughtful feedback, editing, and suggestions. I would not have been able to finish the book without him.

Because family was a recurring metaphor at both Kedma and Fenway, I would like to acknowledge my family. I would like to thank my children,

Rotem and Omri, who listened patiently to my stories about Kedma and Fenway, and my grandchildren, Dahlia and Matan, who showed me the importance of care. Lastly, I would like to thank my wife, Michal, who provided me with honest feedback and supported me with great patience and love.

The stories in *Teachers as Mentors* describe the student-teacher mentoring relationships developed in programs at Fenway High School in Boston, Massachusetts and the Kedma School in Jerusalem, Israel. Aram Ayalon's carefully chosen narratives describe the successful ways that schools can use a mentoring model with a focus on strong personal one-to-one relationships with a range of different mentors. In both schools student performance, attendance, graduation rates, and acceptance to college improved significantly. The author offers us a way to think about reform that is too often ignored. In our effort to respond to the current "crisis" talk we too often ignore what is most powerful: the role of human relationships and learning. These two schools started with what matters most, and redesigned the rest around it.

Mentoring is at the heart of all human learning from the moment of birth. We learn from those we grow up with and from those whom we expect to become like. As we explore our own bodies and surroundings we respond—spontaneously and deliberately, developing greater control over both our responses and the ways in which they are connected to those who care for us.

Schooling is just an artificial extension of this learning—an attempt to organize institutions that do what communities and families once naturally engaged in. But oddly enough society designed institutions that are quite different from the child's prior natural mentoring environment. In the home world there are many mentors, experts at adulthood, and a few mentees who are just working out how to become such adults. The adults are generally going about their own business of living—and the learner is generally imitating aspects of what he or she sees, and looking for clues and cues along the way. The young gradually take on more responsible roles as they move toward adulthood. This is the long apprenticeship we traverse from birth and, in some ways, until the very end of life.

Why we distrusted such a setting as a sensible way to learn to read, write, study history, do mathematics, explore science, and learn other subjects is a long story. Neither this book nor my own experience suggest such institutions are harmless or useless, but they offer plenty of good reasons to make them more—not less—like the environments in which we've learned so much before and after school.

We flourish best with a variety of mentors—including virtual ones (movies and books, for example)—but we know that the most powerful mentors are those with whom we are directly in touch—literally. Children may hear adults speaking standardized English for hours each day, but the language they first talk in and sound like is the one their physically present caregivers speak. Even if they spend only a few hours a day speaking in the child's presence—that's who the child learns from and identifies with.

The success stories that resulted from the programs at Fenway and Kedma are similar to the success students achieved through mentoring at my own schools. Central Park East began as an elementary school—one of two in East Harlem to explore more effective approaches to teaching and learning. In 1985 we started a Secondary School where parents, students and staff worked at Central Park East to try to match the needs of adolescents. We were doing work that had few predecessors—we had few mentors for our own adult work. We knew we needed time for the faculty to work together. We "invented" a community-service program to give the faculty a morning off once a week. We hired one woman to place 80 youngsters (grades 7 to 10) in work settings with interesting adults while their four teachers stayed back at school to work together. We assumed it would do no harm.

Years later, in exploring Central Park East's success, we discovered that over the four years these "outside" adults cumulatively had an impact that we had never known about. These adults helped students find good summer experiences, wrote important reference letters to the colleges, and provided guidance outside of school. Not to mention that they learned skills and habits that were easier to learn "on the job." Based on this discovery we did something shorter and more intense in 11th and 12th grade. This time we paid attention to the kind of work setting that students thought they wanted. The results were similar. It's odd that we were so surprised.

We had forgotten that our model within the school was based on the same idea: Young people needed to be part of a community that included adults—co-members with somewhat different responsibilities. Modern life makes this more, not less, important as schools have tended to become larger and more impersonal, except for a special few students whose learning and behavioral difficulties absorbed more than average time from adults, and the most academically gifted). Schools need to make up for what society no longer provides.

Besides, it has become obvious that a democracy needs adults accustomed to the responsibilities that come with membership in a community. And kids need to see themselves as members of many communities, some that overlap and some that don't.

We ignore what Ayalon has to say at our peril. This is a book that takes us step-by-step through schools that were carefully designed to make it as easy as possible for teachers and students to learn from each other and from their shared world. Following the spirit of the examples presented here, specifically tailored to individual settings, might transform schools into places not only of achievement in scholastics, but also settings where students and teachers enjoy their work together. Yes, a "crisis" of sorts exists—but it's the one that the author addresses: building communities where we all see ourselves as teachers and learners sharing community together.

Deborah W. Meier
Senior Scholar
New York University
Steinhardt School of Education

INTRODUCTION

The 2001 No Child Left Behind Act (NCLB) and the 2009 Race to the Top (RTP) program are recent government initiatives that were created to attempt to close the gap between disadvantaged urban and minority students and suburban middle-class White students. NCLB's approach to closing the gap is through holding schools accountable to students' performance on state standardized tests. Students' test scores, including scores of economically disadvantaged students, minority students, students with disabilities, and English Language Learners subgroups must meet Adequate Yearly Progress (AYP) benchmarks and if not met in six years will result in severe consequences such as school closing and restructuring. RTP also attempts to push schools to improve by providing competitive grants to states that promote such aspects as choice, charter schools, and assessment of teachers based on student performance. Similar to NCLB, RTP also specifies severe consequences to schools that failed to meet AYP through such sanctions as replacing the principal and half of the staff.

So far, NCLB has failed to live up to its promise and the impact of the RTP initiative is too soon to assess. For example, a recent study of 19 districts and 42 schools in five states found that restructuring schools that failed to meet AYP had mixed results and no single reform guaranteed success (Jennings, Scott, & Kober, 2009). One reason may be the lack of focus on creating strong student-teacher relationships. In schools where there are strong student-teacher relationships, students will excel academically and will even take standardized tests seriously because they do not want to disappoint their teachers. As this book demonstrates, one important way to establish close relationships in schools is to assign an adult school member to a small group of students where that adult becomes their mentor or advisor. Although more schools are using mentoring or advisory schemes (using various titles), little is known about the efficacy of such innovation. Starting in the 1960s and continuing into the 1970s and 1980s, the middle and small school movements have incorporated mentoring into their programs but have failed to fully implement it; and little systematic research has been performed on those initiatives. Currently, many schools are introducing mentoring into their school curricula, but research provides few guidelines about exemplary practices.

This book describes two similar and successful youth mentoring models used by two nationally acclaimed urban high schools that have consistently achieved exceptional graduation rates. The book provides a detailed description of their methods based on extensive observation and interviews with teachers, students, administrators, and parents. Using their similar teacher-as-youth mentor and youth advising models, these two inner-city schools— Fenway High School in Boston, Massachusetts; and the Kedma School in Jerusalem, Israel—have broken the cycle of failure for the student populations they serve: children from underrepresented groups living in impoverished troubled neighborhoods that provide few resources.

Students at both schools excel academically, rarely drop out, and go to college in significant numbers (Fenway has a 90% graduation rate, with 95% of graduates going on to college; Kedma outperforms comparable urban schools by a factor of three to four) (Boston Public Schools, 2009; Markovich, 2006). Both schools have won numerous awards, with Fenway High School gaining Pilot School status in Massachusetts, a recognition the state reserves for exemplary schools; and Kedma School being declared one of the 50 most influential educational endeavors in Israel.

The success of both schools is directly attributable to their highly developed teacher-as-youth-mentor programs that embody an ideology and mission that put students at the center of their programs and structures. The models are closely integrated with the curriculum, and support the social, emotional, cultural, and academic needs of students, as well as develop close mentor-student-parent relationships. The model further includes extensive support for mentors themselves.

Apart from the model's potential to narrow the achievement gap, these two schools have a record of creating a school climate that promotes safety and reduces the incidence of bullying and violence. At the heart of both programs is a school community—between departments and functions in the school; and among teachers, staff, students, and parents.

This book is divided into five parts. Part one reviews the current literature that addresses the need for nurturing schools, from varying perspectives: the at-risk youth, the school, the teacher-student relationship, and mentoring. Chapter 1 focuses on at-risk youth and causes of student dropout in the United States and globally, especially among minority students. It also addresses why caring schools are needed now more than ever before. Chapter 2 builds on chapter 1 by reviewing the literature about caring schools, especially in reference to minority students in urban areas, and the importance of creating close relationships between students and teachers. Chapter 3 reviews the youth mentoring literature and its impact on students, especially minority and at-risk students; on the importance of teacher-student relationship and the case for teachers as youth mentors; and on school structures that provide for closer relationships between teachers and students. Chapter 4 describes the backgrounds of the two schools used as case studies, provides brief histories of each school, and explains how the role of the teacher as mentor evolved.

Parts two through four are similarly constructed. Each part opens with an introduction, which is proceeded by two chapters—one on each school—and concludes with a summary and synthesis section that illuminates the similarities and differences between the schools. Part two focuses on the mentoring or advisory classes in both schools including the curriculum, teaching strategies, and approaches. Part three centers on individual teacher-student mentoring by describing the nature of the relationship between the mentors and the students and how these relationships were developed at both Fenway and Kedma. Part four explores school-wide elements that support the sustainable mentoring system at both schools, including the role of teacher leadership, extension of mentor-teacher contact, mentor meetings, co-mentoring, and mental health professionals.

Part five provides a summary and implications of the findings of this research. This section summarizes the benefits of establishing a mentoring system for students, teachers, and schools as a whole; lists important principles to follow; as well as highlights the barriers to overcome when attempting to implement such schemes. Finally, this chapter considers some implications for further research in the area of teacher-as-youth mentors.

PART ONE

ESTABLISHING NURTURING SCHOOLS

I

YOUTH AT RISK AND
STUDENT DROPOUT

Although there are important exceptions, as a group urban high schools fail to meet the needs of too many of their students. . . . Dropping out of school is but the most visible indication of pervasive disengagement from the academic purposes and programs of these schools. (Committee on Increasing High School Students' Engagement and Motivation to Learn, 2004, p. 2)

In their book about youth at risk Brendtro, Brokenleg, and Van Bockern (2002) suggest that "contemporary society is creating a growing number of children at risk for relationship impairment" (p. 12). They further claim that the nuclear family is ill equipped to address youth problems and that it is the larger community that needs to create a nurturing environment for children. Schools, especially in urban areas, are communities that could provide the most support for children, because they engage in ongoing, long-term relationships with children.

However, schools, especially secondary schools, tend to deemphasize relationships between teachers and students and focus more on academic achievement and teaching the subject matter. Such an approach often leads to a high dropout rate, expulsions, and academic failure, especially in schools that serve minority and poor students (Balfanz & Legters, 2004; Steinberg, 2002). Each year about 1.25 million students drop out of school, more than half of them from minority groups. In 2008, while White and Asian American students had about an 80% graduation rate, Hispanic, African American, and Native American students had 58%, 55%, and 50% graduation rates, respectively (Editorial Projects in Education, 2008). Furthermore, over 50% of the dropout rate is concentrated in 2,000 urban high schools where only 60% of the 9th graders finish 12th grade (Balfanz & Legters, 2004).

No Child Left Behind further exacerbates the dropout rate. As schools emphasize high-stakes testing and base their curriculum decisions on test scores, teacher-student relationships tend to become more distant, and students' affective aspects are further neglected (Akos, Brown, & Galassi, 2004; Chambliss, 2007; Gayler, 2005; Vogler & Virtue, 2007).

The high school dropout rate presents an enormous problem both for students and for society. The overwhelming majority of students who drop out of high school fall to the bottom 20% of family income. In 2005 the average high school dropout annual income was $17,299 as compared to $26,933 for a high school graduate. In addition, the likelihood of these youths being imprisoned or on public assistance increased dramatically (Amos, 2008).

A recent national study of 500 students who dropped out of school found that the major reasons students did not finish school were boring classes; teachers' low expectations; academic failure; lack of sufficient structure; and personal hardship circumstances such as getting a job, becoming a parent, or helping family. Many of these reasons were linked to the lack of close and supportive relationships between teachers and students (Bridgeland, Dilulio, & Morison, 2006).

In the same study, when asked what could be done to reduce the likelihood of their dropping out, most of the students felt the schools should provide more academic support to struggling students, do more to protect students from violence and enforce classroom discipline, and provide more individual attention. Many students felt left out or ignored; only 56% of students said they could go to a staff member for help, and only 41% said they could talk to an adult in school about personal problems. In addition, fewer than half of the students said that their schools contacted them or their parents when they were absent or had dropped out (Bridgeland et al., 2006).

Research on interventions with at-risk students suggests that a key factor in reducing dropout rates is encouraging and facilitating student identification with school by providing for close connections among adults and students in the school, involving students in school policy and management decisions, and providing students positions of responsibility in managing school activities (Finn, 1989; Garibaldi, 1992; Newmann, 1981; Sanders, 1996). Similarly, research on student bonding with the school found that when students felt more attached to teachers, more committed to their school, and stronger about their school's norms, they were more likely to have higher academic achievement and less deviant behavior (Payne, Gottfredson, & Gottfredson, 2003).

In the same way research on resilience in schools indicates that there are three elements that protect students against dropping out: "person-to-person connectedness, opportunities for participation and contribution, and high self expectations" (Brown, 2004, p. 83).

In sum, there is an urgent current need to establish school environments, especially in schools that serve primarily minority students, that enhances close relationships between teachers and students and that encourages student identification with and feeling of belonging to a school. This book focuses on creating such an environment through establishing the role of teachers as mentors to students. The next chapter reviews the literature on school conditions, especially in urban areas, that enhance as well as impede the creation of nurturing and caring schools.

2

CARING SCHOOLS

Suppose education had been planned and school systems constructed by people whose interests and responsibilities focused on the direct care of children. (Noddings, 1992, p. 44)

Generally, children perform better in nurturing environments. In discussing the factors that reduce youth violence, Prothrow-Stith and Spivak (2004) indicate that society needs to "create a protective and nurturing context in which all young people can grow and develop" (p. 65). They further specify that the way children are treated at home, at school, and within the community has a significant impact on their success in life. Recent research found that schools that establish a climate where students feel connected to adults, teachers, and peers may lead to a higher retention rate and better academic achievement (Anderman, 2002; Nelson & Debacker, 2008; Osterman, 2000). Furthermore, when students feel that their school is a caring environment they tend to perceive their relationships with teachers more positively (Fredriksen & Rhodes, 2004).

Supportive adults can enhance a youth's social capital. Social capital is defined as "a product of the social environment that when present or available increases the probability that individuals will achieve desirable outcomes" (Woolley & Bowen, 2007, p. 93). Supportive adults also play a key role in the research-based Learner-Centered Model. This comprehensive model, aimed at increasing student motivation to learn, identified building positive personal relations and meaningful connections between students and adults in the schools as key in addressing students' needs in today's schools. More specifically, at the secondary level student motivation to learn was significantly enhanced by creating positive relationships between students and teachers and by establishing a caring climate (Weinberger & McCombs, 2003).

Closely related to the Learner-Centered Model is the concept of Social and Emotional Learning (SEL). SEL is defined as the "process through which children enhance their ability to integrate thinking, feeling, and behaving to achieve important life tasks" (Zins, Bloodworth, Weissberg, & Walberg, 2004, p. 6) and is an important factor in children's success in school. Research suggests that caring relationships between students and teachers significantly enhance SEL (Walberg, Zins, & Weissberg, 2004).

However, caring schools are usually the exception. Most students do not experience close and meaningful relationships with their teachers (Lempers & Clark-Lempers, 1992). Moreover, relationships between students and teachers seem to deteriorate significantly when students transition to middle school, where students report increased mistrust in teachers and decreased opportunities to establish meaningful relationships with teachers (Wentzel & Battle, 2001). The deterioration of student-teacher relationships also corresponds with a decline in students' intrinsic motivation to achieve.

The transition from middle school to high school provides further barriers to creating caring schools. Increased class size, test-focused curriculum, and reduced contact between teachers and students all create barriers to teacher-student bonding (Fredriksen & Rhodes, 2004). These barriers are crucial, as the most important factor that affects adolescents' school adaptation is the degree to which students believe their teachers are supportive and caring (Wentzel & Battle, 2001).

Because the concept of caring in schools is so important, it is worthwhile to examine the nature of this phenomenon and the research that has been done on this issue. Noddings (1992) indicated that caring is a basic need of humans and defined it as "a connection or encounter between two human beings" (p. 15). Benard (2004) identified a caring relationship as "conveying loving support—the message of being there for a youth, of trust, and unconditional love" (p. 44). She further portrayed a caring relationship between adults and youth as comprising respect, a sense of compassion, and active listening and getting to know young people in non-judgmental ways. Caring relationships were found to be key contributors to resiliency among children who survived trauma and sexual abuse (Benard, 2004). They are "the very bedrock of all successful education and . . . contemporary schooling can be revitalized in its light" (Noddings, 1992, p. 27).

Noddings (1992) identified several factors that contribute to creating caring school environments. First, schools should have a stable environment and should provide continuity of place, people, purpose, and curriculum. For example, she proposed that the school day be organized to focus on caring by using the lunch period, a time usually used to give teachers a break from students, as an opportunity for teacher-student bonding. Second, schools should be small enough to allow teachers and students to get to know one another. Third, schools should allocate part of the school day for learning about themes of caring such as how to treat one another ethically. In sum, Noddings believes that teachers need to be educators first and specialty teachers second.

Research on the impact of communal school organization confirms the importance of creating caring schools. Communal school organization refers to creating a caring and supportive relationship among teachers, administrators, and students; creating common goals and norms among these groups; and achieving a sense of collaboration and involvement among school members (Solomon, Battistich, Dong-il, & Watson, 1997). Schools with communal organization benefited both teachers and students. In such schools, teachers experienced higher satisfaction, morale, and efficacy, while students had lower dropout rates and less misbehavior, as well as higher academic motivation, self-esteem, and academic achievement (Payne, Gottfredson, & Gottfredson, 2003).

Research on student intellectual engagement also supports the idea that students need to feel connected to school. Intellectual or school engagement is defined as students' psychological engagement through interest, motivation, and feeling of connectedness to school, as well as behavioral engagement through attendance, participation in educational activities, effort, and social interactions (Woolley & Bowen, 2007). Students, especially minority students, who feel connected to teachers and peers tend to view schoolwork as meaningful, have more positive academic attitudes, and are more satisfied with school (Committee on Increasing High School Students' Engagement and Motivation to Learn, 2004). A large study of school climate based on how teachers rate the climate found that teachers in schools with higher academic performance in reading and mathematics reported positive relationships with students and lower levels of disruptiveness and safety problems. Furthermore, the study found that other measures of student academic achievement were consistently related to teachers reporting greater peer sensitivity, better teacher-student interaction, and a lower level of disruptiveness and safety problems (Brand, Felner, Seitsinger, Burns, & Bolton, 2008).

Additionally, a survey of about 8,000 at-risk middle school students in 50 schools found that the number of supporting adults students had in their lives had a significant impact on their level of engagement. Overall, it is evident that a nurturing school climate and a community that fosters student engagement and bonding is essential to successful student development, retention, and high academic achievement.

A caring relationship between teachers and students is most important in urban schools. In a three-year study of five inner-city Philadelphia middle schools, most students indicated that caring teachers were key to their academic success (Wilson & Corbett, 2001). Students, all of who attended the lowest-performing schools in Philadelphia, almost unanimously defined caring teachers as those who refused to allow them to fail. These students wanted teachers who were willing to become deeply involved with their learning and who accepted no excuses for failure. These caring teachers, according to the students, pushed them to succeed, went out of their way to provide them with help, explained things until they understood, used a variety of activities, understood students' circumstances and incorporated them into their teaching, and were able to control student behavior while also focusing on teaching.

Another study, which investigated small learning communities in urban schools in California and Massachusetts, found that schools with a culture driven by strong bonds or "personalized" relationships between students and teachers enhanced students' academic achievement, respect for teachers and peers, and agency in shaping their status in school and future expectations. Furthermore, close and meaningful relationships between students and teachers helped students overcome personal and social problems and reduced racial tensions among various groups (Conchas & Rodriguez, 2008).

A third study investigated the experiences of 11th and 12th grade students attending a small alternative school created for the purpose of dropout prevention. The school had 127 students and 8 teachers and had a 90% attendance rate as well as a 90% graduation rate as compared to a 50% attendance and graduation rate in the district as a whole. Interviews indicated that students felt an affinity to their school in direct contrast to the alienation they experienced in the schools they previously attended. The major contributing factors to school bonding were the school's small size, caring environment, and individual attention students received. Students felt that close relationships with teachers affirmed their academic ability and that the school offered them space to grow and feel ownership (Swaminathan, 2004).

Therefore, it is important to examine school models that have been successful in fostering a caring climate. One such model is the School Development Program (SDP) based on James Comer's theory that assumes that interpersonal relationships within a school and its social climate must be cultivated before it can enhance academic achievement (Comer, Haynes, Joyner, & Ben Avie, 1996). SDP is a program that suggests a school structure reform that attempts to improve the school climate by forming three teams—the School Planning and Management Team, the Mental Health Team, and the Parent Team. All three teams must work together to promote children's development with an emphasis on inner-city minority children. An example of such care was illustrated by an 18-year-old student in one of the schools that used Comer's model where he had to miss several months of school because he was recuperating from a gunshot wound. The Mental Health Team at the school worked with the student and his family to provide ongoing support through the school's counselors and psychologists as well as through at-home tutoring to enable the student to graduate on time (Haynes, 1996). The SDP model is now used in hundreds of schools and has been successful in raising numerous school success–related factors including academic achievement, and improving classroom behavior and attendance (Borman, Hewes, Overman, & Brown, 2003; Comer et al., 1996).

Overall, caring school models are characterized by teacher-student relationships that provide for support, respect, active listening, compassion, and getting to know students closely in a non-judgmental way. Furthermore, caring relationships play a pivotal role in enhancing student academic achievement, social capital, SEL, and intellectual engagement. A caring school climate is enhanced where the school is small and when there is continuity of people, place, and purpose; and where the curriculum provides for teaching about caring. Finally, caring school climate is especially effective in urban schools.

3

MENTORING AND TEACHER-STUDENT RELATIONSHIPS

Mentoring is a brain to pick, an ear to listen, and a push in the right direction. (John C. Crosby, founding executive director, Uncommon Individual Foundation)

As previous chapters indicated, creating nurturing and caring schools is crucial to reducing student alienation and dropout. One of the most promising of the school programs that facilitate a nurturing school climate is teacher-youth mentoring, also called *advisory*. Advisory programs were initiated in the 1960s and have recently become more widespread among secondary schools (Bogen, 2007). Despite the widespread use of such programs, they rarely last. A survey of middle schools found that only about 20% of the schools fully implemented advisory programs (Galassi, Gulledge, & Cox, 1997). Furthermore, little in-depth research has been done on the efficacy of such programs (Anfara, 2006).

A mentor is defined as an adult who nurtures, supports, and cares for individuals or a small group of students (Rhodes, Bogat, Roffman, Edelman, & Galasso, 2002). The mentor acts as a parent figure to students by meeting with them to talk about social, personal, and academic issues; by working with parents to enhance their support for their children's schooling; and by being an advocate for the students in the school. One of the mentors at Kedma, a case study in this book, described the essence of the mentor's role in the school this way:

He [the mentor] comes home to visit them. He knows their parents. He knows their teachers. The teachers report to him. They [the students] feel that everything is centered on them. This gives them a feeling like an egg surrounded with cotton—with warmth, love, empathy, and a million other things.

Furthermore, mentoring is a very important role for teachers of color as they engage with students of color. Irvine (1989) suggested that Black teachers' role should be that of mentors:

> What seems to be a more appropriate and needed role for black teachers is that of mentors. . . . Mentors are advocate teachers who help black students manipulate the school's culture, which is often contradictory and antithetical to their own. They serve as the voice for black students when communicating with fellow teachers and administrators; when providing information about the opportunities for advancement and enrichment; when serving as counselors, advisors, and parent figures. (p. 53)

In a large six-year longitudinal survey of about 15,000 students, including 1,700 African American students, Wimberly (2002) found that African American students were less likely than their White peers to form meaningful relationships with teachers and that those who were engaged in close relationships with teachers had higher educational expectations and post-secondary participation. The study recommended implementing programs, starting at the middle school level, to foster bonding between teachers and all students, especially African American students.

Regarding mentoring programs for disabled and at-risk students, the Check and Connect intervention program was found to promote school attendance, academic engagement, retention, and improved individual education plans by merely using mentors called monitors (Anderson, Christenson, Sinclair, & Lehr, 2004; Christenson & Havsy, 2004; Sinclair, Christenson, & Thurlow, 2005). While this model does not use teachers as mentors and does not provide mentoring to students schoolwide, it is instructive because it incorporates components that are deemed essential to effective mentoring. The "check" aspect of the model involves ongoing assessment and monitoring of students' school engagement using such indicators as attendance, suspensions, grades, and credits. The "connect" component uses individualized intervention focused on creating a close relationship between the monitor and the student in partnership with school personnel, family members, and community workers (Sinclair et al., 2005). Close relationships between monitors and students are developed through three components: persistence, continuity, and consistency. Monitors focus on maintaining high expectations for their students by refusing to give up or to allow students to be distracted from learning. Continuity is achieved by having the monitor work with the same students and by getting to know their families and educational backgrounds over several years—including summers. Consistency is achieved by monitors providing a continuous message of care, belief in students' ability to succeed academically, and the need to stay in school (Christenson & Havsy, 2004).

Current studies indicate that mentoring programs, most of which use community volunteers, can positively impact youth at risk and minority students by improving grades, enhancing peer relationships, reducing drug and alcohol use, reducing school dropout rate and truancy, discouraging teen pregnancy, reducing school violence, and strengthening parent-child relationships (Dappen & Isernhagen, 2005; Darling-Hammond, 1997; Krovetz, 1999; Watt, Powell, & Mendiola, 2004). However, some studies found that mentoring programs do not positively or negatively impact students (Hickman & Garvey, 2006).

Researchers noted that teachers are rarely used as a source of student mentoring and nurturing even though they spend a lot of time with students (Pianta, Stublman, & Hamre, 2002). When teachers are used as mentors they can substantially impact students. In a six-month intervention study using teachers as mentors to reduce student truancy in a large high school that served an ethnically diverse population in Northern New York, DeSocio et al. (2007) found a significant reduction in truancy among the treatment group as compared to control group. They found that for the students receiving mentoring "the advocacy and encouragement of adult mentors within their school helped forge connections that counteracted social disincentives and feelings of hopelessness and kept them engaged in school" (DeSocio et al., p. 10).

This book features two schools that successfully used teachers in the role of mentors over a period of more than 15 years, rather than for a shorter time. This should enable educators to learn more in depth about the impact of such programs.

Role of Mentoring in Teacher-Student Relationships

Successful mentoring depends on establishing close relationships between adults and youth. Close adult-student relationships were found to be key to growth, learning, and healing in varying contexts such as after school programs, parenting, teaching, mentoring, youth work, and therapy (Noam & Fiore, 2004). Successful youth-mentoring programs were those that established relatively strong relationships between mentors and youth (DuBois, Holloway, Valentine, & Cooper, 2002). One element that contributed to the strength of mentor-youth relationship was the relationship's duration. In a study of 1,138 urban adolescents who participated in a Big Brothers Big Sisters program, Grossman and Rhodes (2002) found that those who had a relationship of a year or longer with their mentors reported the most improvement in academic, psychosocial, and behavioral outcomes.

In the context of teaching, strong relationships between teachers and students are key as well. Data from a nationally representative panel indicated that stronger intergenerational bonding between students and teachers in school was associated with higher academic achievement and a lower likelihood of disciplinary problems, especially for Hispanic American girls (Crosnoe, Johnson, & Elder, 2004). In a study that included interviews with 27 teachers and 117 students in a high school, Bernstine-Yamashiro (2004) found that students' learning was closely connected to how they felt while learning and how they felt about their teachers. In addition, their academic effort was dependent on their belief that the teachers cared about them, encouraged them, and were investing in them. Furthermore, when teachers treated students like humans, created a safe environment for taking risks, and shared their own humanity with their students, high school students' attitudes toward learning improved. The researcher also found that contrary to common belief, students actually wanted close relationships with teachers because they had limited access to parents and other adults. Furthermore, close relationships with teachers helped students work out problems in their outside lives and prepared them to deal with the adult world after graduation. Bernstine-Yamashiro (2004) concluded that teachers who were empathic toward their students and provided them with mentoring were much more likely to reach them than those who did not provide such aspects.

While the importance of the relationship quality between students and mentors is well established, youth mentoring literature is only beginning to explain how these relationships are created. Spencer (2004) suggested that psychotherapy research could provide important contributions to this issue. Heavily relying on the person-centered approach to psychotherapy developed by Carl Rogers (1980), Spencer listed the most important factors that contribute to effective psychotherapy outcomes as follows: empathic under-standing, establishment of warm and positive relations, genuine presence of the therapist in the relationship, and collaborative relations. Similarly, men-tors who nurture strong and positive connections with youth are empathic, are authentic in their interactions, and convey positive feelings toward youth, may be able to create strong bonds with their mentees. Furthermore, Spencer proposed that mentoring might benefit from engaging youth in enjoyable, recreational, and fun activities that establish mentor-youth companionship.

The next section analyzes school structures that enhance teachers' role as youth mentors.

School Structures That Support Teachers as Youth Mentors

Sociocultural perspectives suggest that nested structures in the education sys-tem affect student-teacher relationships. Studies have found that the interac-tion among classrooms, schools, and communities affects the quality of relationship between teachers and students (Fredriksen & Rhodes, 2004). School structures normally do not allow for close student-teacher relation-ships and therefore "a major challenge for schools will be to create settings that can increase and facilitate teachers' and other staff's caring potential, while maintaining academic rigor and teacher autonomy" (Rhodes, 2001, p. 117).

The most important structures in successful school-based mentoring programs were small schools and schools-within-schools where innovative scheduling practices and multiyear teaching were used. These arrangements enable schools to provide students and teachers more time to spend together and nurture long-term teacher-parent-student relationships (Rockwell, 1997). Through observing small schools, researchers found that effective small schools tended to have, among other characteristics, personalized envi-ronments where each student had an advisor who operated as an advocate and liaison with parents, social services, and the community. Advisors also met with students in advisories throughout the week to help students focus on academics, problem solving, and team building, as well as to mentor stu-dents and provide for sustained relationships (Cleary & English, 2005).

Research on urban school reform indicates that the most successful interventions are those that create a personalized environment within deper-sonalized schools. The First Things First (FTF) intervention was designed and implemented by the Institute for Research and Reform in Education in Kansas' schools starting in 1998. Key to creating a personalized environment at the schools were small learning communities of less than 350 students who were taught by the same teachers for several years. Additionally, the model used a family-advocate system—a model similar to the mentor programs established by the schools in this book. In the family-advocate system each student was paired with a teacher or staff member within each learning community who was expected to meet with the student regularly; monitor the social, academic, and emotional development of the student; and serve as his or her advocate. The advocates also served as liaisons between students and parents—helping engage parents in their child's school life. Finally, each advocate also met with his or her students in a group setting for what was called Family Advocacy Period. Results indicated that middle and high school students in Kansas gained significantly in various measures over eight years—including substantial gains in academic achievement, graduation rate, and state test scores while reducing dropout rates (Quint, Bloom, Rebek Black, & Stephens, 2005). A follow-up study calculating this intervention's net return on investment found that FTF was the least expensive intervention when compared to other successful intervention programs and the benefits of the program exceeded costs by a factor of 3.5, saving the taxpayer over $150,000 per additional expected high school graduate (Levin, 2009).

Advocacy, mentoring, and advisories are programs that have been used extensively for over 30 years in middle schools with the aim of creating a caring school climate that promotes close bonding between teachers and students. In studying the characteristics of exemplary middle schools, George and Alexander (2003) found that these schools included effective advisor-advisee programs. However, studies found that advising programs in middle schools had a variety of goals that did not necessarily focus on building adult-student relationships. Some advisories were designed for community building while others centered on developmental guidance. In addition, some middle school advisories focused on invigoration by using fun and informal activities, while others emphasized teaching study skills. Finally, some advisories ended up focusing only on administrative aspects such as relaying administrative information to students, taking attendance, and making such advisory sessions similar to the traditional homeroom period (Galassi et al. 1997).

By examining the barriers to successfully implementing advisory programs, Galassi et al. (1997) found that conceptualization and implementation and maintenance factors were to blame. Conceptually, school staff often failed to agree on the goals of the advisory program and teachers felt that they did not have the skills to implement advisories. Furthermore, researchers found that insufficient care was given to the impact of advisories on teachers' workload. With regard to implementing and maintaining advisories, researchers discovered that there was a lack of ongoing staff development, time allocation for advisories, relevant curriculum for the programs, and support for advisories among parents.

In lieu of the obstacles to implementing successful advisory programs, George and Alexander (2003) proposed the following remedies: school-wide shared commitment and vision regarding advisory programs, intensive and ongoing staff development, small advisory groups, thoughtful scheduling that ensures sufficient and appropriate advising time, and extended contact between advisors and students beyond advisory classes.

Upon reviewing similar successful volunteer-based mentoring programs, researchers drew like conclusions. A meta-analysis review of evaluations of the impacts of mentoring programs on adolescents revealed that the strongest predictors of successful programs were "ongoing training for mentors, structured activities for mentors and youth as well as expectations for frequency of contact, mechanisms for support and involvement of parents, and monitoring of overall program implementation" (DuBois et al., 2002, p. 187–188). In a successful high school pilot program that used the teacher-as-mentor program to help reduce student truancy, the intervention program included extensive teacher support—such as a mentor orientation, a mentor support group, and a full-time coordinator who maintained constant communication with parents and students (DeSocio et al., 2007). Yet, most mentoring programs have neglected to incorporate these factors in their implementation plans (DuBois et al., 2002).

To summarize, mentoring significantly impacts students, especially urban, minority, and at-risk students, by building close relationships between students and adults. However, research on successful models of teachers-as-youth mentors is seriously lacking. This book attempts to fill that void.

4

SCHOOLS WITH TEACHERS
AS YOUTH MENTORS

When asked to describe what makes Boston's Fenway High School special, the staff members indicated: "It's all about relationships." (National
Association of Secondary School Principals, 2004, p. 3)

Kedma School demonstrates what a dedicated and idealist staff of
teachers could generate among students whom society has given up
on. Again we see that through receptivity, warmth, support and mostly
love, it's possible to achieve academic success with almost any student.
(Bar Shalom, 2004, p. 135)

The two schools examined in this book, the Kedma School and Fenway High School, were chosen because both have used teacher-as-
youth-mentor programs for a long time, allowing for extensive
experience in developing and refining these programs. This chapter describes
the context and development of each school, its ideology, and how youth
mentoring fits with the schools' missions, to aid in understanding why these
schools chose these programs and their evolution.

The Kedma School

The academic gap between Mizrahi and Ashkenazi (European Jewish background) students is well documented (Ayalon & Shavit, 2004). For example,
among 1998 high school graduates 36% of Ashkenazi students enrolled in
college by 2006 while only 27% of Mizrahi students did so (Swirski, Konor-
Atias, Kolovov, & Abu Hala, 2008). Kedma was established to challenge this
inequity.

Kedma is a 7–12th grade secondary public school comprising approximately 150 students—one class of 25 students at each grade level—and 13 full-time (defined as 24 hours per week) as well as 9 part-time teachers. Kedma was established in 1994 in a poor neighborhood in Jerusalem by a grassroots protest movement that operated from 1993 to 1998 with the goals of establishing small schools in urban and rural communities that provided students with college preparatory, culturally relevant, and learner-centered educational environments. The movement criticized the Israeli establishment for discriminating against Mizrahi (Jews from the Middle East) children by providing them with inferior schools. The movement's founders felt that the Israeli education system channeled Mizrahi children to lower, non-academic, and special education tracks, ultimately marginalizing Mizrahi history and culture in the curriculum. Kedma's mission is described this way,

> Kedma strives for providing the highest academic level without selection
> and tracking while nurturing school-community relationships. . . . Kedma
> believes that in neighborhoods and development towns, like in the rest of
> the country, most of the youth . . . could reach matriculation and higher
> education level. (Kedma Brochure, 1995)

Kedma chose, therefore, to locate its school in the Katamonim neighborhood in Jerusalem—one of the places that the State of Israel chose to create public housing during the 1950s to settle new immigrants from Middle Eastern countries. Typical of Israel's settlement policies, the government built housing developments that had substandard infrastructure and that segregated Mizrahi immigrants from Ashkenazi immigrants and veteran residents. Most of Kedma's founders grew up in this poverty-stricken neighborhood where they felt their education was substandard. It was this experience that led them to start the school and locate it in this neighborhood.

Because the school is classified as a magnet school, students from the greater Jerusalem metropolitan area could enroll at the school as well. Kedma receives funding similar to other public schools; however, as of 2008, its facilities were relatively inferior to those of other schools—it shared a gym facility with an adjacent school because Kedma did not have one, the library had limited resources that allowed for few new books, and office space was limited so teachers and guidance staff had little privacy. Kedma had a small computer lab consisting mostly of donated computers, but its infrastructure

and Internet capability were limited, thus preventing teachers from fully uti-
lizing the Internet's vast instructional resources.

Despite Kedma's lack of resources and its location in a poor neighborhood where the local high school has a low success rate in matriculation
exam (exams required for college acceptance) completion (typically 8–16%),
Kedma's students had a significant higher success rate in these exams.
Between 2001 and 2007, on average, 46% of Kedma seniors completed
matriculation exams—a rate significantly higher than that of other schools
in poor neighborhoods and development towns in Israel. Additionally, each
year about 20% of Kedma students were missing only one or two exams
for full matriculation completion (Markovich, 2006; Sheleg, 2005; personal
communication, 2008). Kedma's matriculation exam success rate mirrored
the average rate among high school students in the city of Jerusalem (Swirski
et al., 2008). Furthermore, while the average dropout rate of Mizrahi students in Israel as a whole was more than 50% (Zameret, 1998), Kedma had
only a handful of students drop out. The school also became a leader in
implementing critical pedagogy in its curriculum. Consequently, the school
developed a reputation as a model school and a Mecca for educational
researchers and educational innovators (such as Bairy-Ben Ishay, 1998 and
Markovich, 2006). For example, in 2006 the school was chosen as one of the
50 most influential educational endeavors in Israel (Haaretz, 2006).

To achieve the ambitious goal of getting every student to complete and
pass matriculation exams, in turn giving all students the opportunity to go
to college, as well as to empower Mizrahi students, Kedma established several
principles:

> (1) a culturally relevant and interdisciplinary curriculum; (2) heterogeneous
> groups that do not classify students by ability; (3) parent involvement in
> the school administration and decision making; (4) a learner-centered focus
> that provides students such resources as team-teaching teachers who men-
> tor small groups of students (up to 10), small class sizes, and an after school
> program for academic help and enrichment. (Kedma Brochure, 1995)

The school utilized a variety of strategies to achieve these goals. To
achieve a culturally relevant and interdisciplinary curriculum, the staff developed several interdisciplinary thematic courses: Community and Society,
Social Education, and Language and Culture. The curriculum in each course
was designed to allow Mizrahi history and culture equal representation to

Ashkenazi history and culture and reflect the students' experiences. Furthermore, the interdisciplinary courses focused on enhancing critical thinking, social and cultural awareness, pride, and civic values. The curriculum usually required students to conduct projects, and promoted in-depth processing. For example, in the Community and Society course students worked on a school-wide yearlong research project about their neighborhood. Students collected documents and interviewed people in the community about organizations and institutions, history, architecture, and accomplished people. Students who previously held negative views of their neighborhood as a place of poverty, dirt, and crime found that it had a long history of social activism. The student project became the basis for a book about the neighborhood (Yona, 2002).

Additionally, the school used art and theater as opportunities for self- and cultural expression. Kedma has made art and theater an integral part of the curriculum with options to take matriculation exams in these fields. The visual arts teacher, for example, incorporated developmental and cultural material, such as the use of Mizrahi music, to inspire students' work. He said,

> I think that their connections with themselves through art and the development of self-confidence [through the use of art] enabled them to connect more to their roots, to their neighborhood, and to their ethnic membership. . . . For example, in their artistic work you see a lot of influence of Islam. [They use] symbols from Islam: Hamsa [a hand symbol of good luck], flowers, and birds. [These] are Middle Eastern symbols taken from Islam.

Theater was also often taught in order to enhance students' self-expression as well as critical thinking, as the theater teacher said in Markovich (2006, p. 98), "When I work with students I try to deconstruct together with them what is written [in the script]. I ask the students how the characters are represented, who presents these characters, why did he do so, and who is the audience the play is written for."

Incorporating matriculation exams in non-academic areas such as art and theater allowed heterogeneous grouping by deemphasizing students' tracking based on their math or reading abilities. While students were separated into ability levels in traditional academic areas, they had ample opportunities to interact with one another in mentoring and electives courses.

The goal of parental involvement in school administration and decision making was also achieved in deliberate ways at Kedma. Each year, about 30 parents (20% of the families in the school) were involved in various committees and subcommittees. The principal continuously attempted to increase parental engagement by arranging school-related retreats and activities for parents. She acknowledged the need to involve parents in new roles beyond advocacy. A joint parent-school staff leadership committee, run by a facilitator (rather than by the principal), was created to enable parents to have a voice in school-wide decisions. In one leadership meeting, for example, the facilitator talked about the "essential triangle" that was necessary for the school's success—mentors, students, and parents. Discussions with parents often focused on such topics as school discipline policies, building facilities, and policies with regard to parents who cannot afford extracurricular activities for their children. Also, in those meetings administrators were held accountable by providing a progress report about a variety of school issues including success rate in matriculation exams.

Finally, one of the hallmarks of Kedma's success was providing individual attention and support through a mentoring system that has been used since the school's establishment. It is this program that the school deemed the heart of the school and the key to its success. Each class was assigned two mentors (called melavim, or accompanists) who, in addition to teaching classes, conducted a weekly two-hour mentorship class. As part of their teaching workload, mentors receive four hours a week to meet with students individually during school time as well as two hours to meet with students individually, keep in touch with them after school, and communicate with parents. As previously indicated, Kedma received funding similar to other public schools; however, because it was classified as an experimental school, it had a higher level of autonomy to allocate its funding resources and develop its curriculum. Thus, the school chose not to hire full-time school counselors and instead employed various part-time guidance staff to support the mentors' work. Furthermore, it established a Friends-of-Kedma parent advisory board that sought additional funding through grants and donations. The additional funds paid for extra costs, such as additional mentoring hours and assessment of students with disabilities. For example, during the 2007/2008 academic year, $43,000 of fund-raising money was used to pay for six extra hours for each of the 12 mentors and $100,000 for an after school program, as well as smaller amounts of money for assessment of students with disabilities and smaller class sizes (personal conversation, parent advisory board head, 2008).

In sum, Kedma is a small school that was created with an ideology to support and empower marginalized students to pursue college aspirations as well as strengthen their identity and cultural pride. While the school created a variety of aspects to promote its goals, the most important component detailed in this book is the teacher-as-youth-mentor program.

Fenway High School

Fenway High School is a small high school situated at the heart of downtown Boston near Fenway Park—the home stadium for the Boston Red Sox. It is composed of about 300 students in grades 9–12 and 27 teachers. Fenway originated in 1983 as an alternative program for 90 students who were identified as disengaged from school and it was associated with English High School, one of the oldest schools in the United States. Larry Myatt, one of Fenway's founders and its first principal, recalled the nature of the students whom Fenway targeted: "We were a school within a school and our initial population was kids who were dropping out. Or many of them actually were attending a school quite regularly but not attending classes. So that was quite paradoxical. They were coming every day looking for something but weren't finding much."

An important influence on creating Fenway was Theodore Sizer's (1984) publication of *Horace's Compromise* which suggested that high schools alienated students and needed to be reformed by creating small, autonomous high schools where students could get personal attention. Boston school district responded by creating a few experimental programs including Fenway. Myatt described Fenway's basic approach: "We were clear from the beginning [of Fenway] that something was wrong [with the school's structure] and we needed to listen to kids to tell us what their experiences had been that made them unsuccessful." The staff at Fenway engaged in conversations with students and discovered the challenges students were facing in Boston in the early 1980s. As Myatt recalls,

[W]e heard some pretty consistent things of street violence, handgun violence. It was just beginning. That was kind of unfortunately the changeover from fighting without guns to fighting with guns. These were some of the days of the cold war when Reagan came in and there were concerns about whether we're going to have [a] nuclear future; HIV/AIDS was brand new, unknown, mysterious, scary. So listening to the kids, they told us a lot about what could be the basis of our curriculum because they were things that in an emergent way were their topics of interest.

As a result, the founding vision of Fenway was student-centered and was described as follows:

> [A]ll students can learn if they feel safe, are supported by close personal relationships with their teachers, and study relevant, in-depth curriculum that stays in tune with research on human learning and development. Fenway set out to provide a school environment where student needs were at the center of educational practice, and where new programs might be developed to better serve their intellectual and social growth. (Fenway High School website, 2009a)

James,[1] a former student and a guidance counselor at Fenway, vividly remembered Fenway's student-centered focus at its inception:

> They [Fenway's teachers] wanted to know more about us and they were involved in our lives. So, it wasn't us against them anymore. They became someone that we can go to and talk to. Someone we can trust. So, this developed the relationship of what Fenway [is]. . . . It was . . . about building relationships with students and students building relationships with teachers.

Sizer's ideas for school reform further influenced Fenway. In 1989 the Fenway program joined the Coalition of Essential Schools—a network of schools created by Theodore Sizer. The coalition advocated 10 principles including creating a small personalized school environment and in-depth exploration of the curriculum. Fenway sent teachers to observe several schools that were members of the Coalition of Essential Schools and adopted many of the coalition's practices including a teacher-as-youth-mentor program that was labeled advisory. Myatt described that influence:

---

[1] Most names have been changed to protect identities.

> They [coalition member schools] did a lot of talking with each other and sharing and they had very strong advisory programs. What impressed us was that they were so much better at structuring to support students socially and emotionally that the young people could pursue the academics with more enthusiasm.

In 1992, as a result of the teachers' visits, Fenway decided to replace an existing course called Social Issues with the advisory program. Social Issues was created as a vehicle to mix grade levels and to unite teachers with a common, team-taught course. Judy, a veteran teacher, recalled the role of this course in transforming the role of teachers from only subject matter specialists:

> That was the beginning of the idea that you can have a course that really targeted personal development issues for kids. . . . And that's where teachers take on a different role. I am not only teaching science now I am also teaching teen issues.

While the new advisory remained team-taught, it became age specific and the school attempted to keep the students with the same advisors for several grades. Later, in 1995, to further develop a sense of belonging and promote a community of learners, Fenway divided the school into three cohorts or houses where students stayed together from freshman through junior year. Each house had a unique program connected to an outside partner such as the Museum of Science and Children's Hospital. The advisory became instrumental in enhancing partnerships between the school and these outside institutions.

In 1998, after moving to several locations, Fenway settled back in the Fenway neighborhood where it originated and became an independent school. It also gained Pilot School status—a designation provided to exemplary schools within the Boston Public Schools—aimed at establishing models for other Boston schools. This status, similar to Kedma's, enabled the school to have more autonomy and control over its curriculum, staffing, budget, and governance.

Regarding curriculum, Fenway chose a variety of innovations that promoted its vision. It chose to start the school at 8:40 a.m., later than most high schools, because research suggests that adolescents are more ready to learn later in the morning. The school also chose to use block scheduling—four periods of 80 minutes including one double period—to enhance in-depth coverage of material and to reduce student load per teacher (75 students per teacher instead of the usual load of 150) to allow for more personal connections between teachers and students. Similar to Kedma, Fenway created interdisciplinary courses so students could gain deeper understanding of the curriculum. It created a humanities course that incorporates literature, social studies, language arts, and philosophy organized around essential questions while enabling students to explore their own cultural roots. Mathematics was also taught in an integrated fashion. The course integrated a variety of mathematics areas such as algebra, geometry, and pre-calculus with communication skills, cooperative learning, art, business, and the biography of mathematicians. A third example of interdisciplinary curriculum was the venture program for 11th and 12th grade where students developed communication and business skills through working and interacting with area businesses and non-profit organizations. At the 11th grade level students explored current events, wrote position papers, and collaborated with outside organizations to develop business proposals that advanced their own position papers. At the 12th grade level, students completed a six-week internship with the organization of their choosing based on their career aspirations (Fenway High School website, 2009b).

In addition to control over its curriculum, Fenway was able to shape its own staffing to best serve its vision. For example, it chose not to offer programs in art and music and instead hired more guidance counselors to provide more support for students and the advisory. Further supporting the school's autonomy was the creation of a board of trustees, originally created to prevent the district from closing the school. The board, composed of community members, leaders from partnership institutions, parents, students, and teachers, sets the school policies and provides political, economic, and networking clout for the school. The school also had a development officer and volunteers who conducted fund-raising for the various partnerships, curriculum development, and programs. For example, in the 2007–08 academic year, Fenway's budget included $320,000 (12.6% of the total budget) for extra activities, the majority of which was spent on instructional and curriculum review, as well as for student activities, professional development, and administrative expenses (Fenway Annual Report, 2007/2008).

Fenway serves mostly minority students, the majority of whom were at risk of failing or dropping out of school before attending Fenway, and 60% of its student body qualify for free or reduced lunch. In 2008, 42% of the student body was Black, 41% Hispanic, 14% White, and 2% Asian. Nevertheless, on average 90% of the students graduate in four years and about 95% attend college. Furthermore, the school has a very low dropout rate of about 1.5% annually (Boston Public Schools, 2009). The school received numerous awards such as Massachusetts Commonwealth Compass School in 2007 and "a high school where Latino students excel" by the Mauricio Gaston Institute in 2008, and was one of only three schools nationally recognized by the Gates Foundation for its exemplary math program. In addition to providing personalized education and in-depth interaction with the curriculum, the school boasts numerous collaborations with area universities and community organizations. In 2009 it had nine different partners including Boston Museum of Science, Children's Hospital, Dana-Farber Cancer Institute, Harvard After School Initiative, and internship programs with Tufts University and Emmanuel College (Boston Public Schools, 2009).

Overall, similar to Kedma, Fenway is a small school with a clear ideology and mission that puts students at the center of its programs and structure. To promote academic success, it created a curriculum, an advisory program, small learning communities, and other structures to nurture and support students who are at risk of failing and who are mostly from a minority urban background. Since the early 1990s, both schools have experienced a program that puts teachers in a different role—one of a mentor. The next section provides more in-depth descriptions of the mentoring (or advisory) classes in each school.

PART TWO

MENTORING CLASSES

Sometimes we cancel mentoring classes because students have test preparation so they come by on their own and ask, "What about mentoring? What's happening with mentoring? We want mentoring!" (Rami, Kedma mentor)

I don't think we would have been where we're at if we did not have advisory. Because we are so content deep, higher-order-thinking driven in our classes, it doesn't allow the kids to have an oooooh [breathes deeply]. You know the only time they feel that way [relaxed] is in gym. And that's pretty much it. So advisory is another opportunity for that kid to relax a little. (Elisha, Fenway advisor)

T his section focuses on the nature of the mentoring classes established at both Kedma and Fenway Schools. As previously indicated, secondary schools often fail to create structures and a school climate that enhance close teacher-student relationships as well as address the social and emotional needs of students. As this book demonstrates, mentoring classes can play an important role in achieving these goals. For example, the Healthy Kids mentoring program, which incorporated relationship-building and self-esteem enhancement activities for 4th grade students in a midwestern school, was found to significantly improve students' sense of connectedness to school and peers (King, Vidourek, Davis, & McClellan, 2002).

What should mentoring classes do to address student needs, especially for those who are at risk and live in urban environments? As indicated in chapter 3, a review of research on middle school advisory indicated that there was a lack of agreement about the goals of advisory and mentoring programs and insufficient information about what constitutes an effective curriculum for such initiatives (Galassi, Gulledge, & Cox, 1997). The founders of Fenway and Kedma faced the same challenges as they planned and implemented their mentoring classes in the early 1990s. Myatt noted that when visiting Coalition of Essential Schools members, Fenway teachers saw a variety of advisory models:

> Some had it as a place where students could do photography, or debate, or study, or yoga, or yearbook. . . . Some schools had it in a way where there was a lot of academic support—that was the focus. Other schools had it as kind of, I am going to use the word loosely, a therapy group support network. Other places had it as community service or particular research into the community.

At both schools, mentors were initially at a loss about what to teach in the mentoring class. Nurit—a mathematics teacher and one of Kedma's founders—recalled the difficulties she experienced:

> At the beginning I had a hard time with mentoring lessons. I didn't know what to do with the students . . . because I was used to going into [the classroom], I have a topic that I have to teach, I look for a creative way to teach so students understand, and that's it. [That's how you teach] mathematics, you know.

Similarly, at Fenway teachers felt uncertain when presented with the challenge of teaching an advisory class. As Kobi, a guidance counselor, recalled, "At the beginning I think it was [difficult] for many teachers. They asked, 'Well, how do I do advisory? Give me a curriculum.' Because it can become sort of a free-for-all if you're not comfortable with just discussion or orchestrating a discussion or a group discussion. So that could be a challenge."

Part two describes the curriculum and activities used in mentoring classes at both Kedma and Fenway, as well as how teachers and students experienced those classes. It also identifies commonalities and differences between the two schools.

5

KEDMA'S MENTORING CLASS

As previously described, mentoring classes were an essential aspect of mentoring at Kedma. Students attended a two-hour mentoring class every week that was team-taught by their grade-level mentors. This class was student-centered in that it concentrated on the academic and social needs of the students and had become a major vehicle for creating a community in the classroom. The mentors at Kedma had worked through the years to develop activities and curriculum for the mentoring classes that were student-centered. As Nira, a veteran mentor who later became a principal, said,

> We do things in a very orderly manner. There is a structure to the [mentoring] activity [and] there is a theme. . . . We decide on a theme for the year, we collect relevant activities, and we also use situations that happen during [the school year]—these are the most successful mentoring lessons—situations happen [in class] and we talk about them.

Furthermore, mentors continually planned and assessed mentoring lessons. As Gila, another veteran mentor, indicated,

> Mentoring lesson is not something that is done as an afterthought, but it is actually a lesson that Yoni and I sit, think about the goal and how to achieve it in a more interesting and engaging way than other classes. . . . [After the class] we sit, analyze it, and [identify] where we made mistakes and what we should have done.

Clara Yona-Meshumar, Kedma's founder and first principal who now co-directs the Friends of Kedma Association, has recently begun collecting and publishing chapters of a manual that describes the teacher-developed mentoring curriculum at each grade level. So far she has completed the 11th and

12th grade chapters. In the manual she describes the goals of the mentoring class:

> Strengthening self-concept and belonging, acquiring tools for group activities, [and] strengthening students' skills [such as communication, critical thinking, social and political awareness, and goal setting]. The group will discuss a variety of issues such as: personal and social responsibility, adolescence issues, test anxiety, individual-group relations, gender relations, value clarification, and social and community norms. (Kedma, 2009, p. 3)

To achieve these goals and maintain a student-centered class, mentors insisted that all class members participate equally and be heard. As Rami articulated,

> Everyone talks and no one avoids participation, everyone has a place in class. In the circle that we make, even if someone is absent, there is always a chair to represent the missing student. There are rules for participating so everyone can talk and everyone listens to one another—not just hears but really listens. [The goal is] to create real trust between all members and to know that what is said [remains confidential].

As students were expected to listen to one another and participate, mentoring lessons provided various opportunities for students to get to know one another. For example, an appointment activity was commonly used across grades. In this activity students made appointments to meet face-to-face with all their classmates during the week and used a set of questions to get to know one another. Students then had to share what they learned about their classmates with the whole group.

In addition to common goals, the mentoring curriculum had different emphases depending on the grade level. Nira described the differences in mentoring class curriculum between lower grades and upper grades:

> In 7th grade, it's the connection to the new place, [it's about] getting to know one another. . . . There are lots of activities [to support] becoming acquainted with other students. . . . [In the upper grades] there is the issue of the matriculation exams and how you prepare for the exams. . . . Toward the end [of school] I realized I needed to prepare them for graduation and to help them manage their relationships [with their peers] so they understand that there is not much time left [to be] together and

[they should] try to get to know one another not [only] on a superficial
level because [some of them] were together since 7th grade and I don't
know how much they really got to know each other.

Lower-Grade Mentoring Classes

As previously indicated, the lower-grade mentoring classes focused on opportunities for students to become better acquainted with one another and
establish a community. Furthermore, lessons focused on teaching students
good study habits and to identify with their new school. Dorit, another veteran mentor, felt that because Kedma had a stigma as a school for dropouts,
it was important to have students "talk about the principles of Kedma so
they will be proud of this place and not ashamed of it." Because younger
students often viewed teachers as adversaries, mentors also had to focus the
lessons on developing students' self-confidence and trust.

To enhance community feelings among students, mentors often took
their classes to have breakfast together, as well as on field trips and other
community-building experiences. Furthermore, activities during mentoring
class reinforced a sense of community. For example, in one activity students
wrote both something true and something fictional about themselves. Students then had to guess who wrote it and differentiate between the fictional
and non-fictional facts. According to Nira the value of the activity was to
"give a picture, a view on someone and you suddenly discover that he is that
way . . . and myths about some children were broken."

To further the sense of camaraderie, mentors often utilized games that
created a sense of fun and facilitated human relations. For example, during
a "ping-pong" activity students threw a ball to one another and shared something positive and something they thought needed to be improved about
one another. Mentors also used ball-throwing activities to assess students'
emotional status by asking those who caught the ball to express how they felt
at school. Often, games were multipurpose. For example, one game required
students to build a pyramid using cups while blindfolded. The activity was
meant to simultaneously help students empathize with disabled students and
learn about persistence and peer interaction dynamics. Games also involved
learning new and personal information about one another. For example, the
mentors distributed wrapped boxes called "happiness boxes" and each student shared what she or he would like to have in the box. The box activity

was also used with other topics such as personal wishes for the new year or what students wanted to get rid of, things they are ashamed of or sorry they did, for Yom Kippur (Day of Atonement where Jews ask for forgiveness for their sins).

Activities were also tailored to address social dynamics and the developmental and emotional issues that preadolescents faced. For example, mentors used "feeling" cards that asked students to elaborate on their feelings by completing statements such as, "When I am sad, I feel . . ." Activities like these enabled mentors to create visual maps of their students' academic, social, and psychological needs and assisted them in making decisions about tailoring instruction to student needs. For example, one mentor said, "I notice that . . . students are not respecting one another. And then, based on where the class is, I build the mentorship curriculum."

Mentorship activities at the lower grade level were also used to raise social awareness. Movies were often used to stimulate meaningful discussions about personal issues. One such movie featured an Iraqi (Mizrahi) child who was considered a slow learner but was discovered to be gifted. The movie described the challenges he faced at home as the one who had to mediate among his divorced parents, problem brother, and neglected grandfather. The students, according to their mentors, were able to identify with various aspects of the child's experience as they themselves experienced similar situations. Follow-up discussions enabled them to further understand their own family situations and develop survival strategies. As Nurit, another mentor, revealed,

[We used this movie] because there are [in the movie] complex relationships as well as guilt and anger. We talked about parent-children relationships and when to take responsibility and when not to, and who is guilty and who is not.

Upper-Grade Mentoring Classes

The 11th and 12th grade mentoring class chapters (the only chapters completed at present; see Kedma, 2009) provide a window to the typical mentoring class activities as well as to aspects unique to upper grade levels. Both manual chapters address such issues as belonging, gender differences and equity, goal setting, and identity. Additionally, because students take matriculation exams in both grades, both chapters focus on helping students prepare to succeed in these exams. However, the 11th grade chapter acknowledges the unique situation of 11th graders as the "sandwich grade" where students are no longer excited about high school as they were in 9th grade, they have completed some matriculation exams, and they are still one year away from graduation. The chapter, therefore, suggests that in order to keep students motivated, mentors should focus on students' main concerns—identity; belonging; and relationships with peers, teachers, and parents. The 12th grade chapter concentrates more on preparing students for life after school. Activities promote goal setting and planning for the future; the process of leaving school and saying good-bye to peers and teachers; and values and issues students will face in life such as serving in the army (mandatory for Israeli non–Orthodox Jews), choosing a partner, and social justice.

Although used in other grade levels as well, a typical 11th grade mentoring activity was photo language (or the language of photos). In this activity, a variety of pictures that depict human relationships were hung around the classroom and students were asked to pick pictures that were most meaningful to them. Through the process of explaining why they identified with these pictures, students got to know one another on a deeper level. The activity was commonly used as a prelude to helping students create their own priorities. Nira described how she used this activity:

> My theme, for example, is the social dynamics in the classroom. So everyone chooses a picture that, from his perspective, reflects the social situation in the class, [also reflects] his social reality, [that is] where he is now in the classroom. . . . And usually the picture gets you to talk . . . so, through the picture you're starting a [discussion] topic.

Nira also mentioned how other topics such as boy-girl relationships and childhood used photo language as an instrument to enhance awareness.

Another common strategy at the 11th grade level involved using poetry to increase awareness of particular topics and generate discussion about them. For example, within the theme of developing a community in the classroom, students were asked to respond to and discuss a poem excerpt dealing with human support: "Things that are given free are most dear, a simple hand, helping shoulder, sharing heart, nurturing soul. The most expensive things don't cost money but they [are] worth a fortune."

Twelfth grade mentoring activities focused more on graduating and planning for the future. One such activity required students to write down what they wanted to achieve in life and how succeeding on matriculation exams would assist them in achieving those goals. Following the writing exercise, students gave each other suggestions for overcoming barriers. Students were also asked to create time lines and concrete plans to achieve success on matriculation exams.

To further explore life goals, students were shown maps of Israel and the world and were asked to describe the farthest place they had visited and how they felt being away from home. Then they were asked to pick among statements that expressed various future options such as stay close to their family and neighborhood or move abroad, and explain their choice. In addition, songs and movies that addressed issues of moving away and exploring life options were shown and discussed. For example, when discussing the issue of military service one mentor chose to show the movie *Hair*—an American anti-war movie. Nurit explained why she chose to show the movie: "We asked them how it [the movie *Hair*] is the same [as] and different [from the situation in Israel] and what they think, because . . . they don't want to enlist in the army."

Another important issue for seniors was graduation. Being together for several years in a small, nurturing environment and spending most of their lives in their local neighborhood, students often feared moving away. Mentorship lessons led students to celebrate the relationships they established with friends and mentors through such activities as constructing a yearbook together, while simultaneously encouraging them to discuss and explore what military service and life beyond might mean to them.

Because Kedma is a 7th–12th grade school, it also includes 10th grade in its upper division. While the mentoring curriculum at the 11th and 12th grade levels focused on preparation for the future, 10th graders generally experienced more discipline issues, partly because students were less mature and partly because there were more new students who transferred to Kedma at this grade level than at any other. Therefore, mentoring activities often addressed student self-control and behavior. Gila described an activity she used to address the problem of students talking back to teachers:

> We talked about the [differences among] thinking, feeling, saying, and doing. We drew a very nice poster and before that we role-played a

variety of real-life school-based situations—all sorts of difficult situations that they face, and [discussed] . . . what they think and feel regarding those situations and . . . what they say and do [in these situations]. We talked about this distinction between what I think and feel [about a situation] is my own, private, personal, that no one could take away from me, and the moment I say and do [something publicly], then there are consequences [that] I need to take into consideration.

Mentoring activities also dealt with gender issues, such as choosing boyfriends and girlfriends, and gender stereotypes. They focused on encouraging students to explore what characteristics they were looking for in a partner. After filling out gender stereotype surveys, students contemplated acceptable and unacceptable male and female roles.

What Students Said About Mentoring Classes

Students commented that the mentoring class was important and influential. They felt that mentoring classes helped them improve personally, socially, and academically. During the mentoring class, students were exposed to one another on a personal and intimate level, which they felt made them a closer community. They heard different opinions and learned to accept others who were different from themselves. For example, Haim noted that he learned about a student who belonged to a Messianic Jewish faith: "[In the mentoring class] we wanted to know about his religion because he believed in Jesus. . . . At the beginning of the year we would not accept him and we used to laugh at him. Now . . . we treat him nicely."

Sharing personal items was another activity that contributed to students' sense of community. Dahlia, an 8th grader, described how a get-to-know activity enabled her peers to understand her family situation:

Not long ago each one of us brought a personal item that we have had for many years. . . . I brought a picture of my father. . . . [W]e passed it around and they asked us why we brought [these pictures] and how it connected to us. . . . My father was in critical condition two months ago and he almost died in my own hands. . . . This [showing the picture] helped, because many didn't know about me. . . . [N]ow there's [better] communication in class.

Dan indicated that sharing personal items allowed his peers to see a new side of him and not just what they saw at school. "[They learned] that there are many more things that I do and they simply don't know. . . . It helped a lot. . . . They changed [their attitude toward me] and they are more interested [in me]."

In the blindfolded pyramid-building activity mentioned before, students also felt they gained new perspectives on their peers. Haim saw a peer he had known for a long time in a new light:

> We had a child who was with me for seven years and he was the biggest troublemaker in class—always pushy and mischievous. . . . We then realized he was smart [because] he knew where [to place] all the cups, but when he got to the last cup . . . he messed it all up. Then we understood that he didn't have patience but he has the brain. He is a good kid.

Indeed, students often felt that mentoring classes unified their class. Dina indicated she enjoyed mentoring lessons because "[they do] all sorts of things to bring us together."

Students also felt that mentoring classes helped them resolve conflicts. Aaron described the conflict resolution process: "Telling the story, what happened, each one tells his side of the story and then they [mentors] say 'let's get it over with.'" Using this process, Aaron was able to resolve a yearlong conflict he had with a female student that culminated with the female student apologizing to him. Aaron learned, "Saying sorry is worth the world."

Several students indicated that the mentoring class activities allowed them to express issues that bothered them. Hanah described, "We would conduct conversations about the class, the [social] situation in class, trips, what was bothering us, and what we felt good about." According to Yair, it provided an opportunity for the students to support each other: "Everyone says what bothers him, he shares it with everyone and then it's possible to help everyone." Through such activities Sarah learned important aspects about her peers: "I didn't know there were children who wanted to be accepted by the group and couldn't because they had a hard time, [for example,] because they were weak [academically] and were afraid the class [wouldn't] accept them." Furthermore, students felt that sharing their difficulties helped their mentors become more responsive. Haim described how his mentor discovered that several students were having difficulties in English and tailored the after school program to help meet those needs.

In addition to helping students support one another, mentoring activities helped students learn more about themselves. Gal, a senior, indicated, "Mentors help you get to know yourself. This is most important. Now, since 10th grade I learned about myself more and got to know myself better." Sarah's comment was representative of students' attitudes toward the mentoring class: "Every mentoring class is important because each one teaches you something different."

6

FENWAY'S ADVISORY CLASS

While Kedma held 2-hour mentoring classes, Fenway's mentoring classes, also called an advisory, evolved into 80-minute sessions given three times a week. However, the advisory curriculum was generally taught in just one session each week, as the other advisory sessions were often used for school-wide functions such as assemblies, or for a study hall with close teacher supervision and support. Although Fenway used the word *advisory* instead of *mentoring*, its advisors' functions were similar to the mentors'. As John, a senior, said, "I would say a good advisor is also a good mentor. I'd say they are one and the same in the school."

As at Kedma, each advisory class was team taught; however, while Kedma only designated some teachers and administrators as mentors all Fenway staff members operated as advisors.

As previously mentioned, Fenway's advisory originated from a multi-grade Social Issues course that all the teachers taught. Another important driver of the advisory's curriculum was Fenway's approach to discipline. Kobi, a guidance counselor and a dean of students in the 1990s, described the school's approach:

> We [Fenway] looked at discipline a little bit differently than it was traditionally looked at. We saw it more of a learning opportunity—how do we teach responsibility versus just dishing out punishments to kids. . . . A lot of times we wanted to work through the issues and get the students to feel that they had a relationship, that they were empowered, and get them to think about different ways of changing the behavior in our schools.

Ultimately, Fenway used the advisory to enhance student responsibility and relationship with peers and teachers. One important tool in creating a community and a culture of dialogue was "circle up." "Circle up means that everybody is going to be in a circle, we're going to have an open discussion; there are certain rules around safety that we're going to follow" (Kobi). Additionally, as with the Social Issues course, the advisory curriculum gave students opportunities to critically analyze social issues and world events and to connect these issues to students' own lives. As Elisha, one of the advisors, described, "[T]hey're talking about issues [sexism, racism]. . . . They are also talking about how that affects them. And they are making connections to their own life." Kobi elaborated on this issue, "If a world issue comes up that we feel connects with the kids, you can take an advisory and really work on it. So, an example [is] . . . the hurricane in New Orleans, the flooding in New Orleans, how does that connect?"

In addition to group discussions, the advisory used writing as an important tool for self-discovery, socialization, community, and skill building. For example, during freshman year students had to communicate with a peer through writing to explain how to make a peanut butter sandwich. James, a guidance counselor, explained, "This is an exercise you have to write as though nobody knows what you are talking about. . . . Don't assume they know what [you're] talking about so be clear with your instructions." During junior year, students were involved in Junior Review—a yearlong process of writing a paper that reflects on their past experiences and sets goals for the future.

Advisory at Fenway also emphasized students' social and emotional needs. A common strategy was to create situations that exposed students' vulnerability. For example, at the junior level Elisha used classroom discussions on sexism and racism "so they [students] are exposing and being vulnerable in front of their group." For 9th graders, James used peer interviews and asked students to share personal values "so, when we're all back together, I want groups to volunteer [to share]. I want you to step out of your comfort zone."

Similar to Kedma, as Fenway's faculty adapted its advisory it engaged in intensive planning that yielded a more structured curriculum incorporating different themes with different grades. Ninth and 10th grade advisory focused on skills and habits that support readiness to learn, and on dealing with issues such as mental health, study skills, time management, sexuality, and nutrition. Tenth grade, however, added a community service component. Kobi explained the rationale: "First [during 9th grade] we have to learn about ourselves and how to take care of ourselves and each other; now [during 10th grade] we can help the community, now we could do the community service piece."

The 11th and 12th grade curriculum concentrated more on college and career exploration. During 11th grade, according to Kobi, students participated in "the Junior Review process where they start processing what they want to do after high school. They put together the major portfolio. . . . That's much more curriculum driven . . . and it's built up to the end of the year." During 12th grade, advisory focused exclusively on preparing for college and future careers through supporting college applications and long-term internships.

The next section describes the advisory curriculum in each grade level in more detail using examples.

Freshman Advisory

The freshman mentoring class was viewed as key to student success at Fenway because it focused on preparing students for the academic demands at Fenway and in-school community building. James described the key themes that guided the freshman advisory:

> We create activities [and] . . . discussions where students learn to work with each other, learn to communicate with each other, learn to resolve conflicts with each other, learn to respect each other from different backgrounds. . . . That is sort of a basic of our 9th grade year. Because we have the different cohorts, we have the different houses and these students are going to be together for three years. So . . . we want to do our best to support that working relationship.

The curriculum for the 9th grade advisory was prepared mostly by Fenway's guidance counselors and revolved around team building; human relations skills dealing with family, peers, and conflict resolution issues; skills important for success in high school such as organization and oral and written communication skills; and critical thinking skills linking current, world, and local issues to personal concerns. Judy, a veteran adviser, provided a more detailed description of the 9th grade advisory:

> So the 9th graders have big units on academic stuff: How do you keep track of your work? . . . How do you talk to a teacher if you need

something? . . . Who are you? . . . All that stuff that can get in the way for
vulnerable younger teens.

The 9th grade advisory curriculum was built around the following themes:

Team building and community building. As previously discussed, advisory
was a major vehicle for socialization and community building at Fenway.
This was achieved by establishing discussion circles, oral and written communication, and sharing personal issues with peers. During 9th grade, students participated in an intensive weeklong experience involving team-
building activities on an island in the Boston harbor "where they are learning
about self, getting through some of their trial tribulations" (James). Other
activities involved creating cooperative groups where students worked
together to solve a problem, such as building a tower using straw or building
a box that would allow an egg to be dropped in it without breaking. The staff
utilized these activities as team-building exercises by discussing such issues as
"Who emerged as a leader? What went wrong? What went right? . . . How
did you resolve the issues? Who did you notice in your groups who didn't
say anything?" (James).

Human relations. Closely related and complementary to cooperative learning and team building, 9th grade advisory promoted positive relationships
among students and between students and parents. For example, one activity
required students to write something positive about each of their peers. One
advisor explained, "If I had 27 kids in there, you could have 27 lines of positive affirmations. . . . I'll never forget this kid last year, who [said], 'I didn't
know that they thought this about me'" (James). In another activity students were presented with a list of value statements and were asked to pick
10 statements, rank them from most to least valued, and explain their
choices. The activity provided insight into each student's internal beliefs and
brought students closer to one another.

Advisory also addressed gender issues among students. For example,
because many students were concerned about sexual harassment, advisory
discussions dealt directly with this issue. As James recounts, "Girls will give
their perspectives—'guys are frowning on me all the time'—and guys will
turn around [and say], 'If you didn't wear that I wouldn't want to squeeze
your butt'. . . . So, we're talking about boundaries, we're talking about
respect." To help students express their feelings about gender issues more

openly, advisors sometimes divided students into male and female groups where students could express their feelings without fear of being judged by the opposite gender.

The student-parent relationship was another issue that advisory covered. James described how family issues were typically dealt with in advisory:

> I had a situation the other day where the male was upset with [his] mom because . . . she had a boyfriend. . . . So, he is upset because at a time he was the head male in the house and now here comes somebody else. So, [we talked about] how [he should] talk to [his] mom and explain to her how [he's] feeling and the changes that [he's] dealing with.

In essence, the 9th grade advisory at Fenway acknowledged that an important component of school success is building constructive relations between students and parents.

Academic-related skills. Freshman advisory emphasized reading, writing, oral, and organization skills that students needed in order to be academically successful. Activities often required students to communicate through writing and interviewing. Furthermore, students were taught basic skills such as how to organize their school bags and how to read instructions. James taught the students organization skills by telling them, "I need you to dump out everything in your book bags. Dump it out. I want you to organize it by subject. Here is your rubber band for your pencils, folders." Students were also given student-decorated agenda booklets that helped them organize their weekly assignments.

Critical thinking using a thematic approach. Finally, the 9th grade advisory used a system (used throughout all grade levels) that promoted critical thinking using the acronym PERCS—Perspective, Evidence, Relevance, Connections, and Supposition. For example, when analyzing Nazism students used a certain perspective (such as Maslow's hierarchy of needs) to explain the source of the rise of Nazism. They then searched for evidence to substantiate such a perspective and made connections to other situations or to literature (such as *The Lion King*'s plot and the relationship between the hyenas and the lion). Finally, they used supposition by examining their own beliefs to try to understand why a phenomenon (like the Holocaust or Nazism) happened and how it could have been prevented.

Overall, 9th grade advisory was deemed crucial for setting a tone of caring and a climate of support, as well as for attaining important skills that could prepare students to succeed at Fenway and beyond. This initial advisory lays the groundwork for the sophomore advisory, which aims to further explore students' identities, and give them opportunities to serve the community beyond the school.

Sophomore Curriculum

Sophomore year advisory curriculum continued to promote community in the classroom by providing various opportunities for students to get to know one another, as well as more in-depth opportunities for students to explore issues that are important to them, such as sex education and self-identity. It also provided students with experience beyond the school walls through community service by being engaged in 40 hours of community service in a community organization or a school. Furthermore, advisory was also used to integrate aspects of the curriculum that would otherwise have been omitted, such as art, technology, and health. Judy described the aspects of the 10th grade advisory curriculum:

> I saw that [10th grade] as the "know yourself/get over yourself year." So the year which we really do go into identity, race, gender—that kind of stuff. I'll be doing a lot of self-expression [and the incorporation] of art because we don't have formal art class. So we push art into the sophomore advisory. And the second half of the year is around community service—serving others.

Javen, an advisor and a math teacher, described the challenges of the sophomore advisory:

> In sophomore [advisory] there is a lot more of "we're still trying to figure what to do with sophomores." How do we support them in their second year of high school—so academic-wise, you know, emotion-wise? How do we get them to really focus and . . . be good students, and take on ownership of time management skills?

One activity that allowed students to get to know each other better, and to explore their own interests was an art project using Photoshop software.

The project required each student to create a representation of his or her face on the computer with half of it covered with objects that represent the student's interests and identity. One student, for example, drew half of his computer-animated face covered with parts of cars to show his hobby and interest in cars.

As at Kedma, Fenway used videos and movies to help students explore relevant issues. In one advisory segment, advisors showed a video of African Americans' attitudes toward shades of blackness, and how lighter-skin African Americans appear to have higher status. Another video showed the obesity problem and obesity's impact on how a person is perceived. In both videos, students discussed the issues and made personal connections to their own experiences.

Students vividly remembered their sophomore advisory. As Ronnie, a senior, recounts, "Sophomore year was a lot of getting to know each other as a classroom and working on projects. Like, we did an art project using Photoshop. . . . We had seminars as well. . . . We all got to share our feelings, unload the stresses. . . . We also talked about drugs [and] sex ed." John found the Photoshop project helpful: "The Photoshop thing . . . certainly helped me get to know my classmates a lot better than if it just [had] been in class because we would talk and share our ideas." Other students remembered the drug education theme where guest speakers were invited. Ronnie remembered that his sophomore advisory had an impact on him by affirming his decision not to take drugs and influenced his friend who was taking drugs at the time to rethink. Ronnie also felt that bringing guest speakers was helpful: "[W]e usually get speakers from outside of school so it's not our teachers, so it's a little easier to talk to them because we don't know them so it doesn't really matter."

While students felt sophomore advisory was useful, advisors felt somewhat unsure about sophomore advisory for various reasons. Cherry, an advisor, indicated that the curriculum was not coherent: "[S]ophomore year is by far the hardest because there is not [a] super set curriculum so it can seem disjointed and kids feel like 'what's the point of this?'" Kobi revealed that setting up the community service aspect of the advisory was difficult:

> Well, it takes some challenges to figure out how to do the community service piece and do it well. Because, depending upon how you do it you are taking the whole group out to do community service together,

which is a challenge. . . . It has to be set up by the teachers and to figure
out logistics.

In sum, sophomore advisory provided students with more opportunities to
get to know one another in depth using various media as well as to explore
the community beyond the school wall. The junior year advisory further
exposed students to life outside of the school and helped with more in-depth
self-exploration.

Junior Curriculum

At the junior level, advisory took a decided turn toward career and exploration of the future, combined with reflections on students' academic and personal past. Students followed a process called Junior Review where they
completed a series of assignments that culminated in an end-of-year portfolio, and a presentation in front of teachers, peers, and family. The school
then celebrated the culmination of this process with "Stepping-up"—a
coming-of-age party for students and parents. Junior Review assignments
included written papers that reflected on past social and academic successes
and failures, interviews with professionals in areas of the students' choice,
and job interviews. For example, in one class students were divided into
groups of three where two conducted a mock job interview while the third
student provided feedback on how well students answered questions. During
this exercise, the advisors circulated the classroom, occasionally stopping the
activity to point out strengths and weaknesses in the students' performances.
The mock interview prepared students for interviews by businesses and non-
profit organizations at the yearly job fair that the school organized for juniors
and seniors.

Another Junior Review assignment required each student to explore a
profession, interview a professional within that profession, and write a paper
describing his or her attitude toward the profession and whether he or she
would consider a career in that field. Students presented their findings to
their peers as a public speaking exercise. Apart from helping students explore
career options, this assignment was supposed to assist them in deciding
where to do a senior internship. Judy suggested that the Junior Review process was a watershed experience:

The kids review their whole academic career, their whole lives, and they create a whole binder of "me" at this point. . . . And that's college prep also. What [are] your choices for college, your first essay? They are all in the binder. They are actually sometimes very touching and very moving. Because they [students] have to say "I sucked, I really sucked [in the past]."

The Junior Review process also helped students look inside themselves. As Cherry commented, "[W]ithin that assignment [Junior Review] comes so much conversation and talk and kids trying to figure out what they are about, and what they like and what they don't like and who they are." Ronnie found the Junior Review process helpful in identifying some of his academic weaknesses:

I guess I had to look at my work ethic. One of the things that I really noticed was my time management. I would get good grades but I would always wait till the last minute and then just pull it off. And that [Junior Review] was really good because I noticed I could just do it early . . . so it wouldn't be that stressful.

Additionally, Ronnie got a close look at his career choice and gained a better understanding of what it entailed: "I kind of knew I wanted to be in surgery, but when I got the real feel for it, like, visited medical schools and stuff, that affirmed it more. But Junior Review is definitely a step up." Furthermore, students often attained a sense of accomplishment after finishing the Junior Review, as John revealed: "I was actually very proud of the end result because I thought it was [an] incredible amount of work for just looking inside myself. . . . I guess I learned about what I want to do in the future. What my true interests are."

The Junior Review final presentation in front of advisors, peers, and family was an emotional event at Fenway. Because the majority of students at the school were African American and Latino pupils who came from poor families in which no one had ever attended college, the Junior Review process gained an additional importance. Cherry described the significance:

[K]ids talking about family issues or, you know, how they are scared about going to college because their family doesn't have any money and they don't know where it will come from. And their older brother had to drop out of school and now he just hangs out in the street. You know, there are all sorts of issues that kind of swirl around.

Observing a Junior Review presentation provided insight into the significance of this process to students at Fenway. Julia, a Latina student from Colombia, conducted her 30-minute presentation in front of her advisors, her principal, several peers, her mother, her sister, and a friend. She called the process a journey where she learned about her strengths and her anxieties about college. Before the presentation began she hung up the Colombian flag to express pride in her identity. Part of the presentation was devoted to her interest in forensic science, accounting, and sociology—areas that she researched and got a chance to explore during college and workplace visits. She also expressed many doubts about the possibility of going to college (in subsequent private conversations I discovered that she was not a U.S. citizen and could not receive public financial support for college). The presentation also included a lecture about specific topics Julia studied throughout the year including important court cases that contributed to achieving social justice in the United States. Following the presentation, her advisors, peers, and principal provided supportive feedback, such as the following advisor comments that highlighted Julia's strengths:

I have so much respect for you. You worked so hard on this. Your writing is incredible. I learned there's nothing you could not do. You overcame some social challenges. Last summer you presented in front of all these teachers. Things are going to happen for you.

The emotional climax of the presentation was when Julia gave her mother a ring as a present for Mother's Day. They both hugged and cried, and her mom said (in Spanish) that she really appreciated all the support her daughter was getting from the school and from the advisors. As we have seen, the heart of the junior advisory curriculum was the Junior Review process that involved specific assignments and procedures that incorporated in-depth reflection on the past linked to exploration of the future in terms of college and job aspirations.

However, some students and teachers felt that the overemphasis on Junior Review shortchanged socialization and community building. Both Ronnie and John felt there was too much focus on Junior Review projects and advocated more variation. Elisha, a junior advisor, felt 9th and 10th grade advisory allowed insufficient opportunities for students to get to know one another: "You can't assume they know each other so much since they changed throughout the years. Ninth graders it's just like 'who we are'. . . . And then in 10th grade it's kind of like they're doing more work-based stuff . . . [s]o it's less community building. Eleventh grade [should] do community building." She also felt students needed more understanding of health issues and, as a result, included in her junior advisory curriculum such themes as who we are, respecting others, showing kindness, praising us, and health themes.

Senior Year

Building on the Junior Review's foundation, senior advisory primarily focused on helping students pursue college and careers through Senior Institute. During Senior Institute students wrote a senior position paper; prepared math, science, and humanities portfolios; engaged in the lengthy college applications process; and participated in a six-week internship.

Similar to junior advisory, the senior advisory curriculum was well structured and focused, as Ronnie described: "What we're doing is college work: working on college essays, filling the common apps (applications), figuring out which colleges [students] should go to." Systematic support for college applications helped close the gap between those who could complete college applications on their own or had home support and those who depended on school help. John compared the senior advisory to structured study hall: "It's more of a focused or organized study hall. . . . Everybody has to be in the same room and the teachers say, 'You know what, this is due, you guys should get this done, if you haven't already, and if you're done with that get this done.'"

The senior advisory also provided a social function. Because students from the three houses at Fenway were combined during senior year, the only time students from each house could get together with members of their house was in senior advisory. As John said, "I see people I don't see normally and I spent two years with them already in the same class. It's nice to be able to come together and talk." Additionally, the advisory provided an avenue for students to share problems and issues they faced. For example, Ronnie described how students had a problem with a teacher giving tests they felt were too difficult, so they used the advisory to bring up the issue and get support from advisors in resolving the problem.

However, similar to the junior advisory, some students felt there was insufficient time allotted to socialization and community building, as Marisol, a senior student, indicated:

> I know especially in my class that would be very helpful, sitting down and saying, you know, what I feel about a certain issue [conflict] that happened in the class. And I think we don't have a lot of that. I don't think we sit down and talk about how we feel about what that person said to that person.

What Students Say About Advisory

Students recognized that advisory was different from "regular" classes. They identified advisory's unique goals, which are to support their academics, to provide opportunities to get to know peers, and to develop a sense of community. Angelo saw the role of advisory positively when he said, "I think it's a good thing to have because it's not really an academic class but it teaches a lot about how to deal with academics." John emphasized the social role of advisory to promote student interaction: "I think advisory plays [a] very big community role so you get to know your class much better. . . . In advisory, it's not a standard class, you can talk, you can help each other work, rather than in class where you [only] pay attention [to the teacher]." John also acknowledged the importance of advisory in dealing with the "stuff" that content-based courses don't deal with: "[W]e . . . get stuff that is not directly related to school stuff, . . . to academics—so . . . , college stuff, career, future stuff, . . . organization stuff. It teaches you the skills that we don't necessarily learn in the classroom." Marisol passionately contrasted discipline-based classes to advisory and compared it to a family:

> You are with your class every day in every single class, but what are you talking about—you're talking about math, you talk about science. But in advisory we get to talk about . . . the person sitting next to me. . . . That's where we actually do talk about our future. [W]hat do we want to be when we grow up? . . . [A]dvisory is just a family.

In sum, the advisory curriculum at Fenway played a key role in helping students successfully transition to high school, build a support network, gain useful academic skills, and become reflective learners with concrete future aspirations.

PART TWO
SUMMARY AND SYNTHESIS

Part two investigated the pros and cons of various mentoring class curricula. Furthermore, in the context of an urban population where students are mostly from minority and low socioeconomic backgrounds, what curriculum meets the needs of students? Examining the common themes between two mentoring curricula that were developed independently and in different cultures may offer a helpful perspective. The elements that seemed to contribute to student success in both programs were as follows:

1. A separate mentoring class

Teachers and students in both schools believed that the mentoring classes were essential to their success and filled a void that regular classes did not address. Teachers in both schools indicated that the mentoring classes enabled them to focus on the social and emotional needs of students, and students, in turn, felt like valued members of a nurturing community. Teachers and students often compared mentoring classes to a family.

2. Teacher ownership

At both schools the faculty developed the mentoring curriculum, which made teachers feel they had ownership over the curriculum. They continuously debated improvements to the curriculum as needed.

3. Preparing for the future and goal setting

Both schools included a significant amount of time and numerous activities that enhanced student reflection, self-analysis, and exploration of future plans. Goal-setting activities often enabled students to realize the relevance of school to their own lives.

4. Student centered

Mentoring activities at both schools focused on listening to students, using movies and videos that were relevant to students' lives, and dealing with students' relationship with parents and peers, gender relationships, and identity issues.

5. Community building

Both schools often put students in discussion circles during mentoring class where all students were listened to and were given a voice. Students had ample opportunities to interact with one another, explore stereotypes, develop interpersonal relations skills, engage in dialogues, and work together to accomplish joint tasks.

6. Differential curricula

Mentoring curricula, while having some common threads, varied significantly across grades. In lower grades (7th through 9th at Kedma and 9th and 10th at Fenway) the focus was on helping students get to know one another and on gaining skills important for academic success. Higher grades focused on preparing students for the future. Teachers at both schools identified grade levels where curriculum was somewhat problematic—at Kedma, 11th grade was perceived as the "sandwich" grade where students were neither at the early and formative stages nor at the graduating level and had to be especially motivated. At Fenway, the 10th grade advisory was seen as problematic because students were not preparing for college yet nor were they new to the high school anymore. In both cases the curriculum provided opportunities to focus on identity and relationship issues.

7. Development of skills and tools for student academic success

Enabling students to use oral, written, and critical-thinking skills was a central part of both schools' curricula. While mentoring did not have specific discipline content like mathematics or science, activities always integrated writing, speaking, and critical analysis skills that were deemed instrumental to students' academic success.

While the mentoring curricula at Fenway and Kedma were similar in many ways, there were also significant differences that are important to point out:

1. Social and emotional emphasis

Kedma devoted attention to teacher-student dialogue and the exploration of social and emotional issues throughout each grade. Activities such as photo language and mapping classroom dynamics became an integral part of the curriculum at all grade levels. Fenway, however, placed less emphasis on social and emotional aspects during 11th and 12th grade and more focus on career exploration through the Junior Review and Senior Institute processes. As noted, some students and teachers in the higher grade levels at Fenway indicated they would like more time for discussing social and emotional issues.

2. Structured curriculum

Fenway's advisory curriculum was structured at the higher grades, for students to accomplish specific tasks. There were also specific benchmarks such as oral presentations and written papers students had to complete. Kedma, however, was less structured. It had a manual of activities but there were no specific required projects and assignments for students to accomplish. Indeed, several Kedma mentors indicated that, although they had become more professional and more organized in their mentoring classes, they still did not have a sufficiently organized curriculum. One mentor said, "There is no mentoring program equivalent to [the] mathematics program or [the] literature [program] and this is problematic."

3. Focus on skills

While Kedma provided opportunities for students to develop oral and written skills, Fenway had a more systematic plan for teaching students how to organize such aspects as their classroom material and how to write a college application.

Synthesis

Mentoring class characteristics at both Kedma and Fenway were similar to features of successful teaching in a multicultural classroom. Landsman and Lewis (2006) identified seven important characteristics of highly successful multicultural classrooms: building relationships and connecting with students, having high expectations, cultural competence, whiteness and White privilege, self-knowledge and reflection, connecting to families and community, and integrating students' lives into classroom activities. Mentoring classes at both Kedma and Fenway were highly effective in building close relationships between students and teachers and among students, creating high expectations for students especially regarding attending college, promoting continuous self-knowledge and reflection among students, connecting activities to students' family life, and integrating students' lives into advisory and mentoring curriculum.

Similarly, Ladson-Billings (1994) in describing case studies of highly effective culturally relevant teaching methods for African American students, focused on the teacher as a promoter of learning and supporter of individual students within a group context. She also highlighted the role of the culturally relevant teacher in honoring students' sense of humanity and self-respect. As demonstrated in this section, mentoring classes at both Kedma and Fenway established curricula that build a community on a systemic and ongoing basis.

Building trusting relationships between teachers and students is also a cornerstone issue in urban schools. According to Ennis and McCauley (2002), developing trusting relationships between teachers and students in urban secondary schools is extremely challenging, but it will probably be successful where students have many opportunities for engagement, positive interactions with teachers and peers, a shared curriculum, and student ownership. Both the mentoring and advisory classes described in this section provided ample opportunities for students to engage and interact positively with one another and with teachers.

Mentoring classes at Kedma and Fenway also provided a space where caring was sustained and built into the curriculum. Noddings (1984) described an ideal caring school environment where caring was not added but built into the fabric of the school. The mentoring classes provided a caring classroom where teacher-student interaction was emphasized, dialogue was essential, and student experiences and goals were considered most important.

PART THREE

INDIVIDUAL TEACHER-STUDENT RELATIONSHIPS

One evening an old Native American man told his grandson about the conflict that takes place in a man's soul. "Son, the internal conflict and struggle are between two wolves that are both in us. One wolf is about anger, envy, sorrow, greed, arrogance, self-pity, guilt, insult, inferiority, and lies. The second wolf is about peace, joy, love, hope, tranquility, modesty, goodwill, generosity, empathy, truth, mercy, and faith." The grandson thought for a moment and asked his grandfather: "And which of the wolves wins?" The old man answered simply: "It's the one you feed." (Kedma, 2009)

K edma's mentoring guide suggests that the mentor's role should be to feed the "empathy wolf." That is, the mentor should motivate students to become positive human beings who are engaged in school. Both schools sought to create nurturing and supportive school environments. Both believed that it was insufficient to invest only in mentoring classes, and necessary to invest in developing direct and personal relationships among mentors, students, and their families as well.

As indicated in chapter 1, secondary schools tend to provide an impersonal environment where students who drop out indicate they do so because they do not have adults in their schools with whom they can talk about personal problems and get personal attention and academic support (Bridgeland, Dilulio, & Morison, 2006). When teacher-student relationships and connections are strong, students, especially minority and poor students, tend to become more resistant to dropping out of school (Brown, 2004). Furthermore, as chapter 2 indicated, close bonds between teachers and students enhance students' social capital, create a more learner-centered school environment, support social-emotional learning, and further students' intellectual engagement. Finally, as indicated in chapter 3, successful mentoring programs depend on the strength of mentor-student relationships. The stronger the relationships the more likely students will succeed academically and socially (Grossman & Rhodes, 2002).

Therefore, it is important to closely examine how close relationships between teachers and students are created. This section describes how teachers at both schools interacted with students individually, and with their families, in their capacity as youth mentors.

7

MENTOR-STUDENT
RELATIONSHIPS AT KEDMA

When interviewing mentors at Kedma they most often discussed the importance of the mentor-student relationship. This theme was expected, because the primary role of the mentors was to support their students by forming close relationships with them. Mentors discussed the social, emotional, and academic support they gave students including regular, in-depth dialogues with students; continuous supervision and monitoring; and ongoing and in-depth communication with parents and families.

Mentor-Student Relationships

From its foundation, Kedma established that providing personal attention to students through mentoring was a priority. The founding principal, Clara Yona-Meshumar, stated, "The success of mentoring is that, first of all, you build a connection with the student—a connection of belonging to the school and to himself." Mentors described their relationships with their students as loving, caring, and close. One mentor said the mentors' main role was to create reciprocal relations with students: "In general, I see the story of mentorship as the story of [creating] a very strong bond [with the student], the story of [creating] a trusting relationship." Knowing students in depth enabled teachers to help students solve their problems. Dita, one of the mentors, used the metaphor of a puzzle to describe her students and explained that the role of the mentor was "to try to get to know the story [of the student], to put the puzzle together . . . to see the mother, father, student, [and] sometimes also the brothers and sisters."

Other mentors treated their students as if they were their own children. Tzvia, a relatively new mentor, said, "The student at Kedma is like your own child. You take care of him from A to Z and the connection is really a good connection." Mentors characterized themselves as "pillars" that the students could lean on, and the ones who "know everything" about their students. In particular, they emphasized their role as listeners. Dorit, for example, described one student who "told me things she never told anyone else." She added, "I felt I provided a safe place for her." Mentors felt that listening and caring for students were essential elements to developing basic, trusting mentor-student relationships—relationships they believed were essential for student transformation. Rami indicated, "I have to accompany them, [I have] to be with them so students can come [to me with their concerns], listen, speak, tell. . . . [This is necessary] in order to create . . . basic trust between mentors and students."

The importance of establishing close relationships between mentors and mentees, in which youth are able to reveal personal information in a supportive environment, is well established in mentorship research (Moore & Zaff, 2002). An integral part of building close relationships with students was having high expectations for students and refusing to give up on them. All mentors stressed their insistence on keeping students on track academically despite obstacles. Dana, a veteran mentor, for example, explained how she refused to give up on a student who was abused at home:

> [You] can't allow the child to fall between the chairs. [And you] can't let him fail in his studies because of all of these things [abuse at home]. We simply enlist the child and the powers that [he] has inside.

The academic support was especially important when students were preparing for their matriculation exams. Mentors provided help sessions after school and sometimes in their own homes. They also had to continuously motivate the students to prepare for the demanding exams and to not give up.

Mentors attributed the close relationships they had with students to dialogues they conducted with them. The next section addresses the nature of these conversations.

The Power of Dialogue

Mentors were allotted four hours of their weekly workload to conduct personal dialogues with their students but often spent many more hours in both face-to-face and telephone conversations with their students. These sessions were devoted to establishing personal connections with students, assessing problems, and meeting with parents and family members as needed. For example, one mentor described a series of meetings she had with a new female student who had frequent bursts of anger: "I made sure to meet her once a week and to check on her. . . . After two or three months, when I felt we established a good connection, I told her it was time to meet with her father."

The mentors found these conversations extremely helpful and insisted on conducting regular dialogue with all their mentees. Several mentors felt that these one-on-one discussions caused them to "fall in love" with their students. Mentors did not, of course, use the term "falling in love" in the sense of boyfriend-girlfriend intimacy, but rather in the sense of creating a caring relationship with the student and his or her family. As Dorit conveyed, "I really fell in love with him [the student] . . . through the conversations with him, with his mother, and dialogue with his father." Mentors also cited various other benefits from these dialogues. According to Tzvia, "The dialogues enable the mentor to show him [the student] that you . . . give him positive reinforcements, [and] to show him that you care about him." She believed that these dialogues enhanced the student's self-esteem and encouraged him to reciprocate the relationship.

Beyond creating close relationships and providing positive reinforcement, mentors saw dialogues as tools for healing. Dorit indicated that dialogues enabled her to "touch the spots that hurt him [the student] in the 'stomach.'" Dialogue also promoted students' self-understanding and enabled them to refocus their energy on academics. Dorit, for example, stated, "Through the dialogues, [the student understood] what was going on with his mother. [Now] he is studying. . . . He likes to come to school." Furthermore, several mentors felt that the dialogues enabled students to reduce their anxieties about taking the matriculation exams. Finally, some mentors found that the conversations with students were also beneficial to themselves. For example, Dorit realized through conversations with students that she shared similar problems and decided she needed therapy.

In sum, many mentors felt that conducting one-on-one conversations with students was essential to their ability to impact them. In addition to dialogues, they emphasized the importance of ongoing monitoring of students.

Students' View of Their Relationships With Mentors and the Role of Dialogue

Students also felt they developed close personal relationships with their mentors. These connections went beyond the relationship established in the classes. As Sarah indicated, "Even if you don't come to class you still can approach them [mentors]. It's like an attentive ear and they also teach you."

Students provided vivid descriptions of personal dialogues they had with mentors and their significance. For example, one female student said, "You can talk to the mentors about everything. I talk [to them] about my social life, my family situation, my academic situation, everything." She went on to describe how the mentors helped her deal with the emotional distress she experienced after breaking up with her boyfriend. Sarah marveled about the advantage of such open communication with her mentor: "To know that if you have something that you can't tell your parents or to anyone else . . . you can to your mentor. It's so wonderful!" Yair compared the teacher-student relationship to a parent-child relationship and reiterated the role of the mentor as a confidant: "[My mentor is] like my second mom. You can talk to her [mom] about difficult things [that happened to you] in school, at home. And if you have some things you don't want to talk to your mom about, you can talk to her [your mentor]."

The influence of personal teacher-student dialogues went beyond helping students deal with emotional problems and providing a listening ear. Students felt these dialogues were transformative. For example, Shir revealed that conversations with her mentors helped her stop smoking: "They spoke to me and this helped me understand a lot of things related to cigarettes and then I decided to stop smoking thanks to them." Dialogues also helped students transform difficult situations at home. Hanah, a 12th grader, related a conversation she had with her mentor regarding problems she had with her family:

> I remember one conversation [with my mentor] when I had a hard time [at home]. I had a mess at home. I had arguments with my mom and my

brother that I discussed with Dorit. She realized I was having a hard time. . . . She clarified the situation for me and recommended several possible alternative [courses of action].

Furthermore, and perhaps most importantly, teacher-student dialogues helped transform student attitudes toward academics. Dina, for example, attributed her increased focus on her studies to her in-depth conversations with her mentor:

Yoni conducted personal conversations with me and told me that I have to study hard because this year we have two matriculation exams. Did the conversations help me study more? Yes. In history, for example, Yoni said I have to study because otherwise I won't succeed. Otherwise [he told me], "like, why are you here?"

Students' transformative experiences at Kedma were even more pronounced because most had experienced cold and impersonal climates in their previous schools. Dina remembered how in her previous school she didn't get help: "In the school I was in, I didn't study. It's like, 'You have problems then keep your problems and don't come.' Here they take [you] and talk [to you about your problems]." Dahlia described how her former school gave up on her: "I simply dropped out there. From the beginning of the year I had academic problems. . . . I would hit [others] all the time. . . . They told me '[E]ither you go to a boarding school or to a school for delinquents . . . or you can go to Kedma.'" She then contrasted that school experience with her experience at Kedma: "In another school [it was] simply, do whatever you can, whatever you know, and leave. They [Kedma's mentors] said, 'No, don't do whatever you can, do *more* than what you can.'"

In summary, mentor-student dialogues, in addition to mentoring classes, were key to establishing a supportive climate for students. However, mentor-student relationships went beyond dialogues; mentors were also assigned the role of student progress monitors. The next section will elaborate on this responsibility.

Continuous Monitoring

All the mentors felt that it was essential for them to be continuously available to students and to monitor their students' progress. Nurit shared, "I go [to

the classroom] in the morning. I see that everyone is present. . . . [After class]
I ask the teacher how it went. I ask the students how things are going."
Another mentor summarized her involvement as lasting "five days a week
from 8:00 a.m. to 2:00 p.m."

As previously mentioned, student monitoring also involved constant
communication with teachers. Nurit expanded, "They [teachers who are not
mentors] provide us information. We talk to them daily. We check when
they [students] have tests, the results of the tests, who took the tests and who
did not, and who got what [grade]."

Continuous student monitoring involved ongoing, two-way communication with parents. Indeed, research suggests that mentor and teacher effectiveness requires communication with multiple people involved in the child's
environment, especially parents (Ferguson & Snipes, 1994; Hargreaves &
Fullan, 1998).

Communication with parents took several forms. Mentors called parents
after school to discuss students' problems, and at the same time also received
calls from concerned parents sometimes late in the evenings. For example,
Nurit revealed, "If a mother calls at seven in the evening and she is hysterical
. . . what options do I have? I can't tell her, 'Sorry this [time] is not
convenient.'"

In addition to phone calls, mentors made home visits. These home visits
often provided new insights. As one mentor said, "There's nothing like what
your eyes see." Dana recounted the impact of such home visits: "All the time
he [a student] says, 'I wish I was an orphan.' . . . When I visited his home, I
discovered that there was . . . violence—there was hitting [going on]." The
mentors indicated that home visits enabled them to get to know the parents,
the surrounding neighborhood, and the students' lifestyles.

The mentors felt that communicating with parents was essential for solving their students' problems. By involving parents in a joint problem-solving
process, they were able to help students transform their lives. For example,
Dana helped a mother become more assertive with her son by helping her
realize she was perpetuating his misbehavior. He was a child who was con-
ceived after years of infertility treatments, and so she was reluctant to
demand that he be accountable for his actions. Similarly, Dita described how
inviting a father to the school for a meeting led her to discover that he was
deformed by skin burns, thus exposing a student's secret. Coming to terms

with this enabled the student to make an important step toward focusing on academics.

In summary, mentors at Kedma saw that their primary role was to create a close relationship with their students. They became the experts and authority figures on their students and their students' families. Students felt that mentors knew everything about them and were there to help them with their problems and challenges.

8

ADVISOR-STUDENT
RELATIONSHIPS AT FENWAY

The whole piece about the relationship [between teachers and students] for me, it's a beautiful thing. But as a professional educator it's a means to an end. It means fulfilling my job here, which is to prepare them [students] for what comes after high school. It allows me to push them a lot harder and farther academically than I would if I hadn't established that relationship. (Danny, an advisor)

This statement by Danny, a teacher and advisor well known at Fenway for his dedication to his students, characterizes the Fenway High School motto—a school that supports teacher-student relationships in order to promote students' success beyond high school.

As Myatt, Fenway's founding principal, indicated in chapter 4, creating a relationship between teachers and students was made possible by establishing a school environment that listens to students. Listening and establishing close teacher-student relationships was also deemed key to students' motivation to succeed academically on standardized tests, as Judy indicated:

I know you don't care about the stuff but do it for me. Will you . . .? Not [only] the MCAS [Massachusetts Comprehensive Assessment System], anything. Anything you do. You don't like school, you can't read, you hate writing, you never read a book in your life. Doesn't feel like something you want to do, but let's try it.

Similarly to Kedma, Fenway also made student-staff relationships a high priority. Comparing the relationship between students and school staff to that of a family, Kobi, a guidance counselor and advisor, indicated, "We're going to know each of these kids, we're going to know pretty much everything there is to know about them. We're going to support them so they can

73

feel part of this [school] family and the caring, loving, and nurturing that's going on." Likewise, students felt their relationships with their teachers and advisors mirrored family relationships where the children worked hard in school to make their parents proud. As Tasha reported, "It's more like a parent-child relationship. You [are friends] with your parents, but you do things to not let them down because they want good things for you."

As Javen said, the advisor's main role was to make sure that "at least here [at school], there is a strong sense of 'Like, I have at least one or two people that I know [and] I can go to. It's part of their role to be my advocate.'"

Three themes seem to characterize teacher-student relationships at Fenway—availability, informality, and advocacy.

Availability. When visiting Fenway High School the close teacher-student relationship was immediately apparent. Even before the school day began, students visited teachers in their classrooms to chat. During lunchtime, the teacher's lounge was empty because most of the teachers ate lunch with students in their classrooms. After school hours, many teachers and students remained in the building until closing time. Students appreciated their advisors' availability. As Liliana pointed out, "I talk to him [Mr. Smith] a lot, like about five times a week, I don't know, I talk to him a lot on the phone."

Danny made the connection between time commitment and a caring relationship: "What does it mean, you know, 'I really care [and] I want you [the student] to do well,' if you leave the building at 2:35 p.m. every day and you get here at 8:40 a.m. There is this disconnect between your words and your actions."

Informality. Complementing the teacher availability to students throughout the day was the informal relationships teachers established with their students. Judy characterized Fenway's school climate as relaxed and contrasted it with the tense relationship in other schools:

> This is a very congenial school. . . . The kids, overall, treat each other pretty well. The teachers treat the kids well. Most days you get a good feel in the class. People just relax with each other, and [are] funny, and there is not a lot of that tension that can come with these schools that are very safety conscious and security conscious. And that comes in part from just the way teachers treat kids from the minute they get here.

Students often sought one-on-one contacts with their advisors as opportunities for sharing. As Cherry, a mathematics teacher and advisor, described:

"They'll [students] just come by at the beginning or the end of the day and kind of talk to me about how, you know, dad had to leave [the] country and they don't know if they have enough money. You know, just a place to debrief because they feel comfortable sharing." Kobi felt that creating informal bonds with students was a more effective model for treating students in need than the traditional clinical approach: "[An] outpatient clinical setting doesn't fit the need [of students] as much because you're just doing an hour or couple of hours [working with children]. . . . So forming the relationship with the student and **being around them** [Kobi's emphasis] . . . day-to-day is a better setting."

Students acknowledged the informal nature of their relationships with their advisors. Ronnie described a typical beginning of the day at Fenway: "When I come to school we don't get straight into work. Like, in the morning [we say], 'How was your day? It was pretty good, what did you do?' stuff like that."

Advocacy. In addition to close, informal relationships between students and teachers and relations that expand beyond the classroom, advisors felt they had a role as student supporters. Javen gave an expanded description of his role in supporting his students:

> We try to be at least one of their, you know, really strong advocates for whatever it may be—if it's talking to another teacher, if it's talking to the administration; also, if it's talking to people outside the community.

Javen elaborated on the advisor's advocacy role as one of a mediator:

> If something should go down between a student, your advisee, and, say, another teacher, sometimes you're expected to be an advocate for the student and to sit down with both the student and teacher and say, "Okay, we need to have a mediation session."

Cherry gave her advocacy role a different meaning—one that empowers students: "We really encourage them [students] to advocate for themselves. You know, if you feel overwhelmed, come and talk to us. That doesn't necessarily mean that we're going to change the deadline, but we do want at least to hear you and talk to you and process through that with you."

Students also felt their advisors were their advocates. For example, Marisol appreciated how her advisors were advocates for her future career: "I had never had a teacher sit down and say, 'Okay, let's talk about your future, let's talk about what **you** [emphasis added] want.'" Liliana pointed out how her advisor opened new opportunities for her: "He came last year [and] he told me, 'Oh, what do you want to do in the summer? . . . I have this really good [program]. . . . It's summer math . . . and you get to learn and they teach you how to think.' . . . So, he brings so many opportunities to you. . . . I love that."

Students' View of Their Relationships With Advisors

As indicated previously, both advisors and students characterized their relationships as frequent, relaxed, and supportive. Students provided more vivid and in-depth descriptions of the nature of their relationships with their advisors.

Personal, social, and academic advising. Students often indicated how their advisors addressed elements in their personal and social life that interfered with their academic success. For example, Tasha revealed that the previous year her advisor helped her regain focus on academics: "[My advisor asked,] 'Do you really think that working every day is playing a role [in why] . . . you are lacking in your classes? You think that [working] is that important?' So I cut some of my working hours." Tasha's advisor continued supporting her the following year when she started socializing too much: "Like lately, I was coming [to school] late. And he [my advisor] basically sat down with me. He asked me, 'Why are you doing this? Why are you coming late?' I was kind of joining a clique. He talked to me about that." Similarly, Liliana indicated she was failing science because she was spending too much time on her social life: "It was more like I focused more on my social life [than my academic life]. So he [my advisor] told me that I had to find a way to balance out [my] social life and [my] academic life. When it's time to party you have fun. . . . When it's time to work, it's time to work."

Close relationships. Students also described their relationships with their advisors as close using metaphors of family and friendship. For example, Angelo had a very close relationship with his advisor. As he described, "Ms. T. . . . is my advisor and I feel really close to her to that point where you know when she's a teacher and when she is your friend. So, I think that's, like, really important. . . . That it's, like, vital to have that connection." The close relationship between students and advisors enabled reciprocal support as well. John indicated that the close relationship he had with his advisee enabled him to help her: "I developed [a] really close connection to her. I can tell when she is angry, or angry enough, which is a lot safer for me. So, you know, I know what I can talk to her about it." Liliana felt her advisor knew her in depth so he could better understand how to help her: "He gets to know, like, your brain, like, really deep inside. He gets to know what are your strengths and what are your weaknesses. And what I really like is that he focuses on your weaknesses and he tries to make [them] into strength[s]."

Advisors' Relationships With Parents

An important ingredient in a close advisor-student relationship is a close relationship between advisors and parents. At Kedma, mentors maintained ongoing communication with parents as an important element in addressing students' social, emotional, and academic needs. Similarly, Fenway established that a key part of the advisor's role was keeping liaisons with parents. Kobi stated,

> Your role as advisor [is] to contact those parents, to let them know . . . my [school] number, my home number, [and] my e-mail. If anything comes up that I should know about or [be] concerned [about], please let me know. [If] they are going to be coming sick. [If] you want to check on how they are doing, please contact me. I am your point person.

Kobi further explained why Fenway has assigned two advisors to each advisory for the specific purpose of enabling closer relationships between advisors and parents:

> Because then you can, as co-advisors, you can really establish [a] close relationship with at least a small group of those students . . . 12 or 13 students. They are **your** [emphasis added] students. To communicate with their parents . . . you're going to know their parents a little better.

Some advisors and students indicated that advisors established close relationships with parents. For example, Marissa described how her mom and her advisor established a close relationship:

> My mom knows him [my advisor] more on a personal level. . . . Even
> though my mom doesn't speak English very well, they talk on e-mail and
> whenever she comes for meetings, they talk; and my mom knows that I
> am with him [under his supervision] all the time.

Liliana illustrated how a close relationship between her mom and her advisor
improved her academic focus and also brought her closer to her mom:

> She [my mother] told me, like, "Oh, I talked to Mr. Smith [my advisor]
> today and he feels the same about you working that many hours." So
> she'll talk to me about [it] . . . and the ways I can change it. . . . Once
> they [my mom and my advisor] grew close, me and her grew close also
> because we can talk about anything [that happens] in school.

In contrast to the exclusive communication channel between teachers
and parents fostered at Kedma, Fenway staff indicated that contact with parents was dispersed among school staff including guidance counselors and
house coordinators. Javen highlighted how these varied contacts worked:
"Advisors are encouraged to communicate with parents as well as teachers.
Depending upon what the issue is, it really [determines] . . . who makes the
communication. If it's something that's affecting all subject areas, the advisor
tends to follow it up. If it's something very unique in one class, the teacher
would probably follow it up." Elisha, an advisor and a house coordinator,
indicated, "Some parents I just send a letter to. . . . I have parents . . . I ask
the counselor to do that or one of the teachers to do that. . . . As long as
there is parent communication it's really not a big deal who does it."

In summary, Fenway created close advisor-student relationships by linking a small group of students to an adult who became the expert on them.
Through establishing a casual environment where advisors were readily
accessible and by having advisors operate as advocates of students, Fenway
was able to significantly enhance student academic motivation. Close contact
with students and their parents enabled advisors to remove personal and
social obstructions to student educational success and motivate students to
engage in school.

PART THREE
SUMMARY AND SYNTHESIS

This section focused on the nature of the relationship between students and teachers at Kedma and Fenway high schools. Part two examined the curriculum of the advisory and mentoring classes and how they contributed to the establishment of caring and nurturing academic environments. However, a supportive and caring school also requires establishing close one-on-one relationships between teachers and students beyond the classroom. Part three showed how both students and mentors perceived their relationship and what aspects contributed to these relationships beyond the mentoring or advisory classes. Teachers and students at both schools shared the following perceptions:

1. Mentor as an expert on students

   At both schools mentors (called advisors at Fenway) were expected to become experts on their students. They were expected to know everything about their students' academic, social, and emotional needs through continuously listening to students, interacting and engaging in in-depth dialogues with them, and maintaining close communication with parents.

2. Family relationship metaphors

   Students and teachers at both schools used a variety of family-related metaphors to describe the nature of their relationships. Relationships were often described as close, informal, and intensive.

3. Time for one-on-one relationships

   Both Kedma and Fenway created time for teachers and students to interact. While Kedma designated time during the regular school day for personal conversations between mentors and students, Fenway's student-advisor dialogues occurred before and after school as well as during lunchtime.

4. Advocacy

   Both schools designated the mentors as advocates for their students. When students had conflicts with teachers, mentors often mediated and advocated for them.

5. Close relationships as key to academic success

Neither school viewed close relationships between teachers and students as an end in itself, but as a means to an end—students' academic success. Close relationships did not mean that advisors became students' friends, but rather they became instrumental in identifying and removing social, emotional, and environmental barriers to academic success.

While there were many similarities between mentor-student relationships at Fenway and Kedma, there were also significant differences:

1. Relationship intensity

While mentors at both schools established close bonds with their students, Kedma's school culture provided for closer teacher-student relationships. Mentors at Kedma provided a greater variety of metaphors beyond family-relatedness. They described themselves as "pillars" of support and "healers" and provided extensive descriptions of the in-depth relationships they established with their mentees.

2. Relationships with parents

Whereas mentors at both schools created close relationships with parents, mentors at Kedma established closer relationships with parents through home visits, ongoing phone conversations, and school meetings. At Fenway, communication with parents was more dispersed because school guidance counselors, house coordinators, and non-advisor teachers took on important roles.

Synthesis

Creating close and nurturing relationships between teachers and students is key to reducing student dropout and enhancing academic success, especially for poor and minority students. Secondary students report that when they have close and caring relationships with teachers they show a significant increase in academic motivation, achievement expectation, school engagement, and positive feeling toward school (Johnson, 2009). Studies of adolescents indicate that their relationships with teachers are crucial because they are less dependent on their parents and rely more on outside relationships to explore personal identity (Steinberg, 2002). Furthermore, a growing number of studies indicate that the quality of the teacher-student relationship is even more important for minority students than for White students because they tend to be subjected to more risk factors in their environment (Murray, 2009). Close teacher-student relationships also play a pivotal role in creating urban high schools that serve as sanctuaries for minority students. For example, Antrop-González (2006) found that caring student-teacher relationships were instrumental in making a small urban school in Chicago a sanctuary for Latino students. In that school, students experienced an authentic caring and family-like environment where they felt protected from outside gangs.

Both Fenway and Kedma created a sanctuary-like environment by engaging students in ongoing dialogues with their teachers and by closely monitoring students' social, academic, and emotional well-being.

PART FOUR

MENTOR SUPPORT SYSTEMS

The setting in which teachers work can make it more or less likely that they will succeed in establishing such relations [caring relations with students] or even that they will try to do so. (Noddings, 2001, p. 103)

This book advocates a new role for teachers—that of a youth mentor or advisor. Teachers are usually prepared to teach their subject matter, but they are rarely taught how to explore students' emotional needs or how to dialogue with students, especially those with extensive needs and whose schools normally fail. What kind of structures did Kedma and Fenway create to enable teachers to effectively mentor their students and to become resilient to this emotionally taxing work?

In her work with mentors at Kedma, Bairy-Ben Ishay (1998) predicted that due to the mentors' overwhelming workload they would eventually burn out. However, 15 years after teachers began mentoring at the school, most mentors were still at the school teaching and mentoring. Similarly, at Fenway, 15 years after the advisory program began, advisory was still alive and thriving despite the multiple roles teachers had to take on.

What is the secret to the longevity of both schools' mentoring programs? Research indicates that school support for reform initiatives plays a crucial role in their success. Success with learner-centered school reform, for example, depended on a school-wide cooperative work environment among staff, administrators, and students, especially in schools that work with minority students (Rallis, 1995). While part two explored how both schools supported advisory by creating a structured curriculum, part four explores the support system at Kedma and Fenway that enabled viable and sustainable youth mentoring systems.

KEDMA'S MENTOR
SUPPORT SYSTEM

As previously indicated, Kedma's main mission was to become a
school that would enable Mizrahi students, a group that has been
marginalized in Israeli society, to succeed in matriculation exams
and attend college. It attempted to accomplish this mission by creating a
curriculum that reflected students' culture, by preparing students for the
matriculation exams needed for college entrance, and by establishing a
student-centered environment through the mentoring program. This chapter describes the structures that Kedma developed to support and ensure the
success of its mentoring program.

Enhancing Mentor Contact Time With Students

Kedma established a schedule of classes and courses that enabled mentors to
have extensive time with their mentees—more time than the students spend
with non-mentoring teachers. In addition to teaching the mentoring class
and being given an extra six hours for one-on-one meetings with students,
mentors taught their mentees in the academic classroom. Furthermore, mentors could teach their mentees in interdisciplinary classes that were offered at
the school. As mentioned in chapter 4, Kedma created classes such as Social
Education, and Language and Culture. These classes permitted teachers to
teach in areas that were outside their certification field, which enabled the
school to schedule mentors to teach more classes to their mentees and have
more contact hours with them. Some mentors had as many as 20 contact
hours each week with their mentees. In addition, the school enabled mentors

to follow their students for at least two years to ensure continuity of teacher-student relationships.

Centrality of Mentors

The most significant source of support for the mentors was the central role that they played at the school. All the mentors indicated that they were the main power source at the school, and even the principal became a mentor. The school showcased the importance of mentorship in various ways. Mentors were given extra pay, leadership positions, and continuous professional development sessions. Gila noted that she got all the resources to become an effective mentor: "I feel that I really get all the necessary conditions [to do my job well]. . . . In general, [this is] the whole idea of Kedma. The principal . . . always says that the mentor is the [main] power." Another mentor said, "I feel I have a lot of power—the power to change, to influence, [and] to make decisions." Dita described the mentors as having the last word and, if the mentor believed in a student, "then everyone had to support that mentor." Dorit described the mentors as "the most significant axis in the school and most of the breakthroughs happened thanks to them. . . . It's important to empower the mentors—they are the top team."

Mentors' importance at Kedma was further cultivated through the mentors' forum that met weekly and where important decisions were made regarding such issues as the academic calendar, the curriculum, and the retention or expulsion of students. The next section explores the important supportive role of the mentors' forum.

Mentor Forum

Noa, a part-time special education resource counselor, described the mentor forum at Kedma as the "holy shrine" and the "oval office in the White House." She indicated that this forum was where crucial decisions were made and where "each mentor could press the trigger button"—that is, each mentor had a veto power on important decisions affecting students. Nurit, one of the mentors, elaborated, "In these meetings . . . most aspects of the school are decided . . . the daily schedule and the yearly schedule, what is important and what is not."

In 1995, in Kedma's second year of operation, a weekly mentor forum was established. A facilitator specializing in organizational development was hired to work with the mentors. This forum became the core institution at Kedma where all key decisions were made. The facilitator ran the forum for 12 years, until 2007, and during her first two years as a facilitator she conducted intervention research and documented her work in a dissertation (Bairy-Ben Ishay, 1998). As the school developed its philosophy and identity, the facilitator felt that it was important to create a forum where the voices of the school's leaders could be heard. The facilitator said, "My main goal was to make sure that all voices would be heard so that voices will not go underground. . . . I wanted to organize people to get used to talking openly at all levels." In addition to open communication, the facilitator felt that the mentors would be able to be more effective if they transcended their understanding of their work beyond their daily operations. She indicated,

> I felt they needed to have, at the beginning, someone who could provide a larger vision instead of just the day-to-day operations. They would always talk in meetings about the "here and now" but I would always try to pull them to look for the meaning of it and how it related to their overall goals, dreams, and personal beliefs.

In turn, the mentors indicated that the facilitator was a model for how to facilitate their own class. As Dorit described, "[The facilitator taught us how to work] with a group, under what conditions, and how to know as a facilitator when to stop [the activity] and when to go on. All the types of [mentoring] activities [came from her]." Additionally, the mentors learned how to employ learner-centered activities. According to Dorit, "We started to do more [activities] . . . around [the students] themselves [exploring such issues as] what upsets me at home, what I like, what I hate, what are my relations with my mother."

As the school evolved and established its identity and philosophy, the forum gained additional functions. Aside from promoting open communication among the mentors, it provided opportunities for mentors to develop and rehearse strategies they were planning to use in the mentoring lessons. Mentors then took turns leading the forum by conducting activities they intended to use with their students. Following the demonstration sessions, they received feedback from fellow mentors. Gila described this process: "Lots of times we do . . . the mentoring activities that we intend on doing with our students. We try to practice what we preach. If we didn't like the activity, why should we use it with our students?"

The forum also served as a support mechanism. As Nurit explained, "Everybody talks about their problems, and it gives perspectives to others, . . . what happens in each class, . . . ideas for activities, and ideas for work strategies." Nira felt she got a lot of support from the group: "There is a feeling of a support group. You bring your problems, you hear what happens to others and how they see things. . . . We learn new ways of facilitating and that's important."

Although some forum time was spent talking about specific student cases, the forum used a more self-reflective approach, as Yoni indicated: "This is our time to discuss test cases and what happens to us when we deal with the children . . . and to analyze the dynamics together."

While the forum was pivotal to mentor success at Kedma, mentors also needed help in the classroom. The next section describes the role of co-mentoring in assisting mentors.

Co-mentoring

As indicated in chapter 4, Kedma assigned two mentors to each classroom to provide ongoing support to one another. Nira described how she plans with her co-mentor: "We try to meet once a week and update [each other] . . . and to check the social, academic, and personal situation [in the classroom]—who needs help, what assignments we have for the following week." Often, co-mentoring provided an important opportunity for professional growth—especially for new mentors. Dorit described how, as a new mentor, she benefited from co-mentoring with Dita:

> She was a model for me. The moment I started working with her . . . mentoring looked very different. Her depth, her personality, and yes, the dialogues she carries with the students, and the sparks of love in her eyes for each student. . . . Through her, I learned to love the students . . . love without limits.

Nurit shared how she continually communicates with her co-mentor: "We talk about how our day was, and what other teachers said and what happened with students. . . . We argue, we agree on what to do . . . and it often takes mutual deliberations."

Mentors felt that working in pairs enabled them to distribute the work-load. One mentor indicated that as many as 10 of her students (almost half) had either a social worker, a psychologist, or a probation officer assigned to them. Having to continually communicate with these adults as well as with parents was more manageable by sharing these responsibilities with another teacher.

However, mentors discovered that working in pairs could be challenging because it required continual coordination and often generated conflicts and disagreements. Mentors had to learn how to work with a partner. As Dita indicated, "He [the co-mentor] has to understand that [when] you work as a couple, sometimes you have to give up, sometimes you have to wait and try your partner's suggestions." Nira explained that co-mentors needed to present themselves to their students with consistency "so we have the same definition, the same assignment. We are working together . . . to be one in front of the class." Because of these difficulties, Kedma added guides to work directly with each pair.

Guidance for Co-mentors

Since 2002, each mentor pair has been assigned their own guide or mentor who has met with the co-mentors weekly, guided them in developing activities and a curriculum, as well as in working on their own relationship as co-mentors. Nira described the role of the guide this way:

> I work with her [the guide] more or less on the mentoring class, on the content of the mentoring lessons, . . . [and] on the relationship between the mentor—that is between the couple, if there are . . . conflicts or disagreements.

As Kedma's governing structure evolved, it created 7- to 9-level and 10- to 12-level coordinators who assumed the role of guides. The most important role for the guide was to provide an outside perspective. Dita, a nine-year veteran mentor when she became a guide, described it this way: "The most important contribution [from the guide] is the ability to come from the outside, to listen to what you say, to notice how you project yourself. . . . An outside guidance person guides you by merely being an outsider. It's like couples' therapy."

Gila believed that the guide's help was essential in preparing successful mentoring lessons: "It helps me and Yoni to prepare mentoring lessons and plan for the smallest details . . . and to present the mentoring lesson in the most interesting way."

The role of the guide provided a new challenge to veteran mentors who found new venues for sharing the expertise they had accumulated. For example, Dita felt her role as a guide was "very interesting and fascinating" and greatly contributed to her professional development. Guides also became important role models to their peers. For example, Dana deeply appreciated her guide: "She is a veteran guide. . . . She is first of all a human being and second . . . I feel she has something to give me."

Despite additional peer support from guides, mentors still needed guidance from mental health professionals when dealing with students who had difficult social and emotional issues. The next section describes the evolving mental health support Kedma created.

Mental Health Support

The mentors' role at Kedma was complex and required mental health professionals to help students resolve their social and emotional challenges. In reviewing the challenges facing all teachers in the new millennium, Hargreaves and Fullan (2000) pointed out that because of the increasing number of fractured families, students need more emotional support from teachers, and in turn teachers need more emotional support. Indeed, mentors at Kedma felt their work was emotionally draining. Gila described mentoring as "a long and exhausting process" that required patience: "[One needs] lots of patience and to know that this is a process, and to know that one day the penny will drop [the student will get it]." Nurit expanded on the causes of exhaustion: "All day long your brain is working. All day you are busy with this, and it's a very tiring job." In short, mentors needed help from mental health professionals for personal help as well as professional advice.

A review of literature on caring schools provided in chapter 2 indicated that one of the most successful models of caring schools in an urban setting involved a mental health team. The Comer model, called the School Development Model (SDP), utilized a team of psychologists and counselors with other school teams to provide a nurturing environment to students who live in urban settings (Comer, Haynes, Joyner, & Ben Avie, 1996).

Kedma saw the value of obtaining mental health support, for between 1995 and 2007 mentors met individually with a clinical psychologist on a bi-weekly or monthly basis. Additionally, in a four-year period from 1998 to 2002, two additional psychologists advised mentors regarding specific student cases. More recently, since 2008, a three-year-long municipality-based mental health intervention team has been working with the mentors and students. The mental health team incorporated a psychologist and a social worker augmented by a medical doctor and a dietitian.

The next section describes the nature of this mental health support and its contribution to mentors' success.

Individual Psychologist-Mentor Sessions

Soon after Kedma was established, it became apparent that mentors needed more support. The forum facilitator said,

> I felt during the sessions that I didn't have sufficient knowledge about how to work individually with children and solve the problems that are brought up. . . . I am not an expert in providing for children family intervention. I am not a clinical psychologist.

As a result, Kedma decided to hire Irene, a clinical psychologist, who helped the mentors through individual sessions. Irene defined her role in three areas. First, she helped mentors understand their students: "To improve the diagnostic skills of the mentor and help him develop an appropriate strategy of working with students in a way that will reduce students' resistance." Irene explained it through the following example: "A youngster who has an unusual bad smell might . . . be telling others not to get close to him. . . . [Analyzing the role of] the smell gave us a more profound understanding [of the child]."

Second, Irene helped mentors understand themselves and how their self-perception affected their work with students. She felt that "the more they [mentors] are able to listen to themselves, engage in self-dialogue, and understand what motivates them, the deeper their work with the children [will be] and the more directed toward change." Irene provided this example:

> I can tell you about a youngster who started to steal. The mentor wanted to protect him from school so he wouldn't be expelled. . . . It turned out that the mentor came from a difficult family story of crime at home.

Irene then helped the mentor understand how her own family story affected the mentor's behavior toward her mentee. Irene concluded that "the more they [mentors] are able to listen to themselves . . . the deeper their work with the children."

Third, Irene helped the mentors understand their role within the system so they could be more effective. Irene explained,

> The meeting with other mentors and teachers and the work within the system, which is very intensive there, influences their personal work-space and exposes areas of weaknesses and hurt. During guidance you need to refer to the system and the role of the mentor within it and not just aspects related to the separate mentor's world.

The mentors indicated that the psychologist sessions were helpful. They felt the sessions reenergized them to keep trying to help their students and to look for alternative approaches. One mentor said,

> From my perspective, what the psychologist gives me is to come the next day with a lot, a lot of strength to conduct individual conversations [with the students]. I could give up on the children . . . but she keeps recharging my batteries.

Dita felt that the psychologist got her to face her own limitations, "to sometimes look at the mirror and see horrible and scary things." This honest self-exploration, she felt, provided her with emotional support that reduced her burnout. Nira felt that the psychologist helped her improve her relationship with her students: "I work with her [Irene] on my connections with the children. That is, how to conduct a personal dialogue, and new directions [on how to work with children]. I tell her about problems with the children." Yoni felt that the sessions with Irene enabled him to understand how to solve his students' problems and learn how to dialogue with them: "We bring up various problems we have with students, what it does to us and what we're going through; and second, we learn how to talk [with the children]."

In 2006, after 11 years, Irene's work with Kedma's mentors ended. According to Nira, who became the principal of Kedma, the lack of a psychologist's support had a negative influence on the mentors:

> [A] psychologist's help is still necessary. The previous year there were no personal meetings between the mentors and the psychologist and as

a result the mentors' meetings were much more stormy. When mentors process the problems they have with the help of a psychologist, they come better prepared and calmer.

As indicated, Kedma was able to restore psychological support for an additional three years thanks to the partnership with a municipally based mental health team.

While individual therapy sessions were helpful to mentors, mentors felt they also needed mental health professionals in the school to work directly with students, as well as to guide the mentors as they work with students and parents. The next section explores a four-year intervention provided by two psychologists, who provided their services through a partnership with a non-profit organization.

School-Based Psychologists' Intervention

In 1998 two psychologists began working with Kedma's mentors. They introduced a humanistic approach to student intervention that relied on dialoguing with students. Flora, one of the psychologists, described the strategy:

> The concept [was] . . . that you can free the individual's deep potential. You create areas for growth using tools that are much more focused on the student's world as an individual. It is very much founded on the ideas of Rogers [a known humanistic psychologist].

This approach also emphasized working with the students' families and significant others. The work is further described in Flora's research (Mor, 2003).

The psychologists supported the mentors by a "show-and-tell" approach, as Flora explained: "I decided to take from each mentor one or two cases and focus on them . . . so they [the mentors] will have a real opportunity [to understand how to work with students]." Indeed, the mentors were able to observe firsthand the success of the family intervention approach, as Flora described the work with an Ethiopian student:

> Through conversations with [his] family, we were also able to initiate a conversation with him. . . . The breakthrough came when his older brother said, "But you don't know. He feels inferior, and he feels

unwanted. He feels Black." And then he [the student] was ready to tell his life story.

Through a whole-family intervention, mentors learned how to reach their students more in-depth. As one described, "It's no longer superficial conversations about 'good morning, how are you, how are things.' It's way beyond. It's [about] the complex relationship with his [the student's] parents and how it affects him."

When mentors successfully created dialogues between students and their families they often successfully improved the students' academic success as well. For example, one mentor described how one of her students' divorced parents would not communicate with one another and that the student would not talk to her father. After an extended dialogue the student agreed to meet with her father and reestablish communication with him. The renewed relationship with the father, in turn, led to dramatic improvement in the student's academic achievement.

In addition to family intervention, Shira, the second psychologist, taught the mentors how to diagnose learning disabilities holistically. She explained, "The staff gained, through me, more sensitivity to diagnose learning disabilities. . . . That is, instead of formal assessment using formal test batteries—assessment is process-oriented—you learn about the youngster from a variety [of] points of view."

Through this intervention, mentors gained valuable skills in differentiating their instructional approaches. For example, mentors learned how to create a map of the students' abilities, as Shira described:

Teachers can map their class today with regard to reading, style of thinking, and can informally assess their class and map it as to who can express himself better in writing than verbally. They are [also] more sensitive to specific abilities. Before, they used to generalize and say "this one is a smart boy, this is a slow learner," etc. Today, they have a more analytical understanding.

Indeed, as noted in chapter 5, mentors used a variety of strategies to create visual maps of their students' academic, social, and emotional situations. Most mentors indicated that they knew how to create a profile of their students' strengths and weaknesses and use it to promote student progress.

Dita revealed that the intervention convinced her that working with the students' families was essential: "These things are imprinted in me for ever and ever. That is, the most important understanding is that the child comes from the parents, period!"

Overall, Kedma provided an innovative and comprehensive model, developed over a long time, to support the mentors by focusing on their needs in dealing with students and families. Since Kedma's inception, the mentors' work has been central to the school's mission and has supported the creation of a caring culture. Resources were focused on the mentor program in various ways. While typical public schools have school counselors and psychologists working directly with students, Kedma's guidance staff consisted of outside professionals who supported mentors individually, as pairs, and as a group. Such a system of support emphasizes the notion that the role of mentors is complex and requires extensive assistance (Everston & Smithey, 2000).

However, Kedma's mentors and their supporting mental health team acknowledged that the lack of regular guidance counselors on staff to address the needs of students with severe needs was problematic. As a social worker from the most recent mental health team indicated, "There is something wonderful, amazing in the work of two mentors in each classroom. At the same time we [the mental health team] took care of guidance in the past four years. The school still needs a counselor."

10

FENWAY'S ADVISORY
SUPPORT SYSTEM

As chapter 8 indicated, Fenway's advisors had to listen, make themselves available, advocate for their advisees, and get to know each advisee on a personal level. Chapter 8 also described some aspects of Fenway's environment that contributed to close advisor-student relationships, including co-mentoring, and the supportive role of counselors and house coordinators. Additionally, both chapter 4 and chapter 6 described some of the structures that Fenway High School created to support mentoring, including block scheduling, engaging all staff members as advisors, and establishing three houses. This chapter explores in depth the elements in Fenway's environment that contributed to a successful advisory program.

Enhancing Advisor Contact With Students

Like Kedma, Fenway used scheduling and other structural strategies to extend contact between advisors and students. Block scheduling, which established 80-minute classes, enabled Fenway's advisors to conduct meaningful advisory sessions and lowered their student load. Research suggests that when the block schedule is combined with pedagogical changes it can improve teacher-student relationships (Hackman, 2004). Furthermore, extended advisory time provided the setting for house-wide and school-wide social events that promoted informal relationships among students and between students and advisors.

Another aspect that extended contact between advisors and students was the creation of three houses, or small learning communities, within the school where each cohort of students stayed together for three years. A review of literature on successful small learning communities suggests that providing multiyear contact between students and teachers more effectively creates a personalized learning environment than single-year contact (Oxley, 2007). While teachers could teach students outside of their house, the house structure ensured that students would be more likely to have the same teachers and advisors from 9th through 11th grade. This enabled advisors and students to develop long-term relationships.

Fenway discovered the advantages of the house structure when it created a cohort of students that was linked to an outside partnership. Judy, a veteran teacher, recounted this experience:

> What we realized [was] that "Children's Hospital" kids who were involved in a kind of a cohort that was a little separate from the rest of the school for almost the whole time, the three years . . . actually fared better . . . personally, emotionally, psychologically, and academically than the other kids.

Cherry compared the cohort system to an elementary classroom:

> A cohort of students is together all day [every school day] for three years. So it [is] sort of like 5th grade and you deal with the same kids all day, except here you do it for three years. . . . You are assigned the same teacher freshmen, sophomore, and junior year. So you really develop that relationship.

Javen, a math teacher, further explained the advantage of the house system in enhancing teacher-student interaction:

> I teach in my house and outside of my house. And actually every math teacher teaches in the house and outside of the house, but they teach two different grade levels . . . so the house teachers will teach the majority of the classes [in their house].

Javen also explained that the three-year relationship with his students enhanced his role as a student advocate:

> It really allowed [me] to develop a really strong relationship with those kids—such that [I] became a really strong advocate about their grades

and about other things in their life. [I] could speak and attest to kind of their growth as individuals. Even to this day, that particular group of students, we are really close with because we were together for three years.

Furthermore, advisors indicated that by teaching the same students they advised, they enhanced their effectiveness as advisors. Cherry explained,

It's easier to develop relationships with kids teaching the content actually, and then kind of carry that relationship over into advisory. . . . I mean, I definitely had advisories where there were no relationships because I didn't teach them. And then once I started teaching them . . . they were much more receptive.

While students usually had advisors for more than one year, this aspect of Fenway's program often clashed with teachers' desire to teach at a single level, as Javen acknowledged: "Some people like to stay within a particular grade level. Now, I am really kind of sticking with the senior grade level."

House Structure Support for Advisors

The house structure at Fenway provided further support to mentors through the role of the coordinator and weekly house meetings. Each house at Fenway had a coordinator—a teacher with release time who provided support to advisors. The coordinator organized the weekly house meetings, which served to enhance the teachers' communication as advisors. Also, each house established practices that further enhanced the advisor's role. Javen described the house coordinator's role as follows:

They are kind of organizing things for the houses—events, they match the teams [of advisors], they run the [house] meetings, . . . they also take that role of being another kind of advocate in a sense. So say if a student [is] having problems with all their teachers and their teacher happens to be their advisor, then it may go to the house coordinator that is more removed from the situation. . . . So it's not all the pressure on the advisor.

Advisors found it helpful to have another person mediate between them and the students and parents. Furthermore, weekly house meetings where teachers from different disciplines met enabled advisors to discuss challenges they faced with individual students, as Elisha, a former house coordinator, indicated:

> So on Tuesdays we spend at least 30 to 45 minutes to almost an hour on student concerns. We bring up a student from a certain grade and we talk about that student because you might [have a different] picture than I do. If we all . . . [are] willing to share that then we can put that together . . . to figure out how we should solve it.

Furthermore, Cherry described a flexible system in each house to help struggling students:

> I would say if a student is struggling in science usually it's the science teacher that calls [the parents]. . . . If it's a kid who has trouble in a lot of classes, instead of having five different teachers calling the parents the advisor might say, "I'll be the point person, let me know." Sometimes it's the head of the house. It's not always the advisor.

House policies also supported the advisors. Before each marking period, teachers discussed a selected group of students and wrote a joint narrative to be sent to parents. So, by the end of the year all parents received a narrative. Elisha explained how the narrative process was helpful to her as an advisor:

> It's helpful for the advisor to be there [in the narrative meeting] so he can hear about what else is going on in their classes. . . . Our class advisory, which is much more of a social-type skills class, is different from another class. So, are we connecting with the same observations that someone else is? Are we hearing some of the same patterns and concerns?

While using cohorts as a way to focus Fenway's structure around supporting students helped create a caring environment, Fenway had many students who needed more emotional and social support than one advisor could provide. Like Kedma, it established co-advising where at least two advisors were present in each advisory.

Co-advising

Co-advising provided students with more individual attention and allowed advisors to share the workload and build on each other's strengths. Judy believed that co-advising was key to advisory's success:

> The teachers are also pairs. That, I think, is a key thing—the pairing. It's really hard to do advisory when it's just you and you got to carry the class. We need two people and then you can talk to each other about the kids and you can advocate more strongly for your kids.

Cherry, who advised juniors at Fenway, illustrated how co-advising helped her with the Junior Review workload: "It's nice because there is so much work that comes in to Junior Review. . . . For example, students are researching and writing reflections [about] three different careers each, and they are editing those until they are perfect to go [in] the binders."

Javen described how he and his co-advisor complemented one another:

> Like, she's fabulous with organization and I'm kind of like, yeah . . . I'm here and there and anywhere. Like, kids will get a sense that you got to walk and talk with Javen versus with Carol [where] it's like, "I am going to sit and we're going to talk."

While there were many advantages to co-advising, as at Kedma, advisors found co-advising challenging because of the need for time to develop common policies and a single curriculum. Javen compared co-advising to parenting: "It's more like [a] co-parenting thing where we're addressing it together." Cherry illustrated the difficulty of advising in pairs:

> Obviously, co-advising can be really difficult if you feel like you are with someone who isn't pulling their weight or someone you don't see eye to eye. That can be really hard. That has happened in the school many times.

While co-advising was helpful to advisors, it was insufficient because advisors often needed professional help to deal with students with challenging situations. As at Kedma, Fenway needed extensive support from mental health professionals. The next section describes Fenway's approach to providing support to advisors when dealing with students' social and emotional aspects.

Student Support Team

A key support mechanism at Fenway was the student support team, which was composed of three guidance counselors. In 1994 Fenway collaborated with the Boston school district to create the Pilot School model. As a Pilot-designated school, Fenway gained control over its curriculum, schedule, budget, governance, and staffing. This autonomy enabled Fenway to make choices to help personalize its education, such as hiring more counselors and scaling down other programs. As Kobi explained,

> . . . being responsible for distributing their funds and being in control of their own budget [gave Fenway the flexibility]. So you can afford four counselors if you don't have, maybe, a music program, or you [don't] have an athletic program, or you [do] some additional fund-raising.

Having three guidance counselors on staff to serve 300 students enabled Fenway to give counselors more responsibilities. All the counselors served as advisors for the freshman classes and played major roles in developing the freshman advisory curriculum (see chapter 6). James explained the advantage of engaging guidance counselors in the 9th grade advisory: "It works very [well], especially with freshmen because they are going through changes: interpersonal, development[al], social, . . . health, identity, sexuality. And having [a] counseling background being their advisor, I think, it's very helpful."

Additionally, the counselors served as discipline deans, provided professional development activities for the advisors, and conducted the traditional counselor functions of individual counseling, scheduling, and college preparation. Cherry explained the reason why Fenway chose to invest in guidance counselors:

> In most schools that I have been in your focus is all on content teachers and that's where you put all your resources. . . . And that obviously happened here but we also have . . . counselors who are there to offer guidance, meet with parents, [and] talk to students. There's just a lot of staff [whose] primary job is to be focusing on those relationships and making sure kids are staying on track and not falling through the cracks.

Guidance counselors at Fenway became key supporters and nurturers of the advisor-student-parent relationship. Elisha called the counselors the "depositors of information of students" because "I felt if I had a student concern I could go to the counselors and say what my concern was and they could share insights from other classes . . . or they may know the history of that student since they had the student both years." Because counselors had multiple ways of knowing students, such as through freshman year advisory, from handling students' disciplinary issues, and from maintaining ongoing communication with parents, they became "experts" on each student.

Students felt close to the guidance counselors because they provided them with individual attention. Liliana described how her counselor helped her: "Like, one day I came in and I wasn't having a good day. . . . He said 'Okay, come on talk to me.' And I spent an hour and a half just talking to him. And he found so many ways to help me." Furthermore, students felt that the roles of the advisor and the counselor were complementary. For example, Marisol described how her advisor and counselor fit together: "They both know what has gone [on] with my family and what has gone [on] here socially. But Mr. Smith [my advisor] knows a little more about my academics, while Kobi [my guidance counselor] knows more what I want to be and who I want to become."

Aside from establishing and supporting close relationships between advisors and students, guidance counselors provided professional development for fellow advisors. On staff professional development days, guidance counselors often conducted activities with teachers that illustrated how to promote social and emotional development among students. For example, James described how he conducted group-building activity with teachers:

> The tower building is group work to see who emerges as a leader. What went wrong? What went right? They would be arguing about ideas. How did you resolve the issues? Who did you notice in your groups that didn't say anything? . . . Even though it's a fun activity, they are learning how to work as a group. . . . What we do is make sure that teachers learn it first. I don't know how to do something if I haven't experienced it.

Another professional development activity the guidance counselors conducted was a peer writing critique activity, a common advisory activity. The professional development activity required teachers to critique one another's writing, as James described:

> We [the teachers] did a writing piece where we critiqued one another's writing. . . . [The teacher would say,] "Tell me, how did you get to that? Tell me exactly how to get to that because I don't understand that piece

[of writing]." So now you have different eyes looking at that. It's humbling sometimes, but I think it's really good. It's powerful.

Guidance counselors were also resources for one another, as well as coordinators of mental services from the outside. As Cherry claimed, "So they also serve as counselors [of] counselors. In addition, we have outside mental health counselors who come in [through their coordination]."

In sum, guidance counselors at Fenway were key to supporting the advisors, advisor-student relationships, and students. Cherry summarized their roles:

> They [guidance counselors] do scheduling, but they also . . . either individually [meet] with kids for mental health counseling or [refer] kids to mental health counseling. They also serve as deans basically when there is [a] discipline issue. They are where students are sent. . . . They are advisors as well. They usually advise the freshmen because the goal is to really have someone who is familiar with the culture of the school [and who can] acculturate those freshmen to understand what the values of the school are. They also do all the college [career counseling].

As indicated previously, one of the important functions of the student support staff was to provide professional development to advisors. The next segment elaborates on the type of professional development Fenway provided its advisors.

Professional Development

Every year, advisors met at the beginning and the end of the school year for full-day retreats to discuss and reflect on the advisory. Javen described the nature of these workshops:

> The staff is talking about how we better ourselves. . . . We have opportunity to meet as grade level advisors and talk about common themes and common threads between the three cohorts in that one grade. So we can plan a little bit there, talk about things we have noticed, things we would like to try, . . . or things we would like to do differently.

Fenway also invested in developing and rethinking the advisory by assigning a faculty member to further develop its advisory. Judy described how she was given time over the years to support teacher and advisory development:

I spent the last seven or eight years really working on teacher training. I have had release time to really [make] teacher training a recognizable and desirable phenomenon at Fenway High School. And I also did the curriculum for the sophomore advisory.

While such policies as long-term contact between teachers and students, small learning communities, guidance counselor assistance, and professional development were important to the advisory's success, the school's environment, or climate, can either enable its success or undermine its student-centered approach. The next section further explores the school climate at Fenway.

School Climate

Fenway's leadership created an intentional school environment where students were celebrated and where advisors found multiple ways to interact with students in close and informal ways. Cherry explained Fenway's approach:

I think that most of the student activities help students celebrate some aspects of themselves. . . . [For example,] the Latino heritage assembly is celebrating the Latino heritage . . .'Stepping Up'—it's honoring all the work they have done to, you know, become seniors because at the school there is a huge process you go through the junior year called Junior Review.

The celebrations of students' cultures and achievements involved various fun events that enabled students to relax while interacting informally with peers and advisors. For example, advisory time was often used for school assemblies. Kobi described Fenway's assemblies:

It's one of the good aspects of creating culture and community in the school. . . . Fenway jeopardy became a tradition, which is [a] fun type of competition between the houses. . . . We had Latino assembly last week . . . and they [performed] dances and . . . skits. . . . Next week we have pajama day. We might do decorating. Everybody comes in pajamas and we have fun.

In addition to events in school, Fenway provided opportunities for students to get out of the school and learn in the community. "Project Week" took place two weeks before the standardized test was given in order to raise student morale. Judy explained,

> We know that time of the year is very stressful [because of the Massachusetts Comprehensive Assessment System test] so the teachers are really going to work hard to make this [Project Week] a great week for you. And then kids come back and they are much more congenial about every other task we ask them to do.

Judy described what she did for Project Week:

> We did cultural kitchens—which is learning about food and culture. So, we cooked in Cambridge adult education [which] lets us use their kitchen for free. We cooked Vietnamese food, Dutch food—all kinds of stuff.

In addition to various celebrations and programs, Fenway provided after school clubs that enabled both male and female students of color across grades to socialize and gain additional out-of-school experiences and leadership opportunities. Two counselors started a club for male students of color called Men Organized, Responsible, and Educated (MORE). The program, aimed at the most at-risk students at the school, provided various activities to encourage the students to establish more pro-education attitudes. As Kobi described,

> We do it [create pro-education attitudes] through mentoring. We do it through exposure. We do it through discussions. We do it through opportunities . . . to go places, to visit black colleges, to go [to] events, [and] to go to restaurants. Establishing a culture of males around wanting education for themselves and seeing that "I don't have to be . . . the urban male who discourages education, or doesn't want to focus on [it]. There's different ways for me to be."

The school provided an after school club for girls of color giving them opportunities they wouldn't normally get at home or during the regular school day. Elisha, the program's mentor, described the program:

[We meet] after school once a week on Wednesday[s]. So I order food, we talk about a topic. We laugh. We get to know each other. Throughout the year we go on trips. I take them away out of the state so we get to bond. Some girls, it's their first experience at a specific restaurant or in a hotel or [in] a particular state. . . . We do activities that normally we don't get a chance to do.

While Fenway provided ample support for advisors, several challenges were identified. The next section discusses some aspects that advisors indicated were lacking in Fenway's advisory program.

Advisory Challenges

Several advisors indicated that they had insufficient time to interact with other advisors and co-advisors to share and document their curriculum. Javen suggested,

As far as improving, it would be great if there was a slated time to talk to other advisors. I think that, you know, we, as far as senior year, we're still looking at how . . . our curriculum isn't, like, documented well enough, so having [the] opportunity to really . . . document our curriculum [would help].

Because there were no weekly meetings for all advisors or co-advisors to discuss advising, there were often gaps and inconsistencies. Elisha explained that she organized her advisory curriculum one way but wasn't sure how other advisors organized their curriculum: "I am more structured and it's [my curriculum] mapped [out] for four months. Someone [other advisors] might do something similar to that but it's not as structured and maybe not as consistent." Cherry added that professional development sessions at the beginning and end of the year were insufficient: "All the junior advisors will meet to kind of lay out what the plan [is] for the year. . . . But other than that, you [are] pretty much on your own." The lack of communication between advisors might lead to inconsistency, as Cherry explained: "Occasionally, I'll get a crop of juniors whose advisors I don't feel are doing what they should be doing. Like, we'll have a college fair and the kids don't know anything about it."

Generally, Fenway provided a school environment and support that enabled the advisory to meet its students' needs and cultivate nurturing relationships between students and advisors. Advisor-student relationships were fostered by ensuring long-term and stable relationships between students and advisors through the creation of small learning communities that were continuously supported through staff meetings, house coordinators, and opportunities for fun and educational activities that promoted close, informal relationships. Furthermore, advisors received extensive, ongoing help with parental communication; curriculum development; and student challenges from peers (through co-advising), guidance staff, house coordinators, and ongoing professional development. Though advisors acknowledged areas where they needed more support, such as more meetings between advisors, overall, Fenway provided a system that centered around both students and advisors.

PART FOUR
SUMMARY AND SYNTHESIS

Part four focused on the environment at Kedma and Fenway. The resiliency and long-term sustainability of the teacher-as-youth-mentor programs at both schools suggest that investigation into both schools' "secret" of success would benefit other schools. Comparing both schools shows remarkable common elements:

1. Furthering mentor contact with students

Kedma and Fenway created school structures that prolonged contact between mentors and students. Both schools used scheduling as a powerful tool to ensure that mentors had extensive contact with their mentees both in mentoring classes and in content-specific classes. At Kedma, mentors were paid to make themselves available for six hours a week outside the classroom to meet with individual students, and were given opportunities to teach interdisciplinary courses to the same students and follow their mentees for a number of years. Similarly, at Fenway the house structure ensured that advisors had more contact with the same cohort of students by extending class periods, teaching more classes to the same students, and following their advisees for several years.

From studying Kedma and Fenway, it is apparent that close relationships between teachers and students and the promotion of the teacher's role as a mentor or an advisor could not be possible unless teachers could also develop substantial contact with a small cohort of students for several years.

2. Co-mentoring

Both schools chose to place two staff members in each mentoring class, implicitly suggesting that mentoring classes were more demanding than discipline-based classroom. While one might assume that mentoring or advising classes would be easy, non-demanding classes, both schools approached mentoring as being more demanding than discipline-based classes. Mentoring in pairs enabled mentors and advisors at both schools to share the workload, provide more individualized attention to students, better prepare curriculum for mentoring, and benefit from each other's strengths.

While co-mentoring was extremely beneficial to mentors, it was challenging to match advisors and handle conflicts and disagreements between them.

3. Teacher leadership support

Both Fenway and Kedma created teacher leadership positions that provided ongoing support to the mentors and advisors. At Kedma, some teachers were given release time to act as guides for the co-mentors and meet with them weekly to nurture their co-mentoring relationship and help with planning mentoring classes. At Fenway, some teachers were assigned as house coordinators to help match advisors, contact parents, mediate between advisors and students, and facilitate discussions among advisors about individual students. As at Kedma, the house facilitated weekly meetings among co-advisors and supported their ongoing communication.

4. Social and emotional support team

Both schools valued and heavily invested in support from guidance personnel. Both schools realized that advisors or mentors do not have sufficient tools and professional knowledge to deal with students' emotional and social needs, especially at-risk students. Guidance staff, therefore, became pivotal to mentoring success. Kedma relied on a mental health team of outside psychologists and other mental health professionals who met mostly with mentors but also provided targeted support to the most needy students. Mentors received individual therapy to strengthen their own mental health as well as guidance about handling specific cases and working with parents. The mental health team also provided the mentors with on-site help with the most challenging students including students with disabilities.

At Fenway, due to its autonomy and ability to prioritize its decisions, the school established a student support team of three guidance counselors for the 300 students at the school—a larger counselor-to-student ratio than in most schools. Like the mental health team at Kedma, the counselors at Fenway provided a support system for advisors. They offered advice regarding individual students, support in communicating with parents, and professional development. However, because the guidance counselors at Fenway were fellow faculty members rather than outsiders, they were also involved in the school in other ways, including as freshman advisors, deans of discipline, and traditional guidance counselors.

5. Professional development

Because teachers do not normally have mentor training, both Kedma and Fenway created opportunities, meetings, and workshops to increase advisors' capacity. At Kedma, the mentor forum—a weekly meeting facilitated by an outside professional who specializes in organization development—provided ongoing opportunities for mentors to acquire skills to facilitate mentoring classes, develop common mentoring strategies, develop student-centered school policies, attain support from peers, and work to collectively problem solve individual student cases.

At Fenway, professional development relied more on workshops at the beginning and end of each school year, as well as occasional workshops provided by guidance counselors throughout the year. As at Kedma, it gave advisors opportunities to experience the activities they plan to use with students. Additionally, Fenway occasionally provided specific teachers with reassigned time so they could offer more professional development and support to advisors.

While there were many similarities between the ways Kedma and Fenway supported teachers as mentors, there were also significant differences:

1. The role of the mentor

Although both schools emphasized the role of the teacher as a mentor, they saw its importance differently. Kedma's mentors were a select group of 12 teachers who were considered the school's leadership team. These mentors had significant power in the decision-making process regarding such aspects as student dismissal, scheduling, and curriculum. The weekly mentors' forum became an important decision-making body at Kedma. However, at Fenway all teachers and some non-teaching staff were advisors, but there were no regular advisor meetings to discuss advising issues. Instead, weekly staff meetings were organized around each house (led by the house coordinator), subject matter (math, science, etc.), and whole-school staff (led by the principal). The implication of this differential emphasis was that Kedma's mentors received more support than Fenway's advisors. Furthermore, because Kedma's mentors communicated with one another, mentoring classes were more consistent and more similar in the type of activities they used than the advisory classes at Fenway. As a result, Fenway's advisors sometimes felt they were on their own and did not have a clear idea of what other advisors were doing.

2. Mental health support

Although Fenway and Kedma gave their mentors support from mental health professionals, the nature and amount of support differed. At Kedma, the focus was on helping mentors develop themselves and provide relevant support to students through outside professionals including psychologists and a facilitator. At Fenway, however, guidance counselors who were full-time school staff members and knew the students in multiple ways provided the main advisor support. The result was that Kedma's mentors showed more reflective skills than Fenway's advisors when talking about students and about their role as mentors. However, Kedma's mentors had to rely more on themselves, especially when dealing with difficult students, while Fenway's advisors had more immediate, ongoing, and effective help in dealing with students and their parents.

Synthesis

Part three showed that both Fenway and Kedma created "sanctuary-like" environments where students and mentors engaged in dialogue in close and nurturing relationships. Creating such a student-centered environment would not have been possible without creating a similar nurturing environment for mentors. Part four provided a detailed description of the variety of strategies both schools utilized, in order to create a sustainable and supportive climate for mentors as they engaged with their students. Both schools provided extensive scaffolding including scheduling, teacher leaders, mental health professionals, and frequent meetings among mentors to make it happen. Through this support, mentors gained invaluable skills in how to conduct mentoring classes and interact with students.

When asked what he believed were the most important aspects of building better urban schools, Charles Payne, an urban school reform researcher, said,

> The crucial issue is the degree to which the adults can cooperate with other adults: teachers with other teachers, teachers with parents, with principals. . . . Of the 80-some variables that the Consortium on School Research looked at over its 20-year history, one of the strongest predictors of positive school change has been a collective sense of responsibility. (Heale & Scott, 2010, p. 2)

Working together is not an easy task. Often schools, especially in urban settings, suffer from low morale, a top-down administration style, and lack of resources. However, both Fenway and Kedma utilized numerous structures, professionals, and resources in their schools that enabled mentors to work together to establish close relationships with parents and students and promote students' academic success.

PART FIVE

SUMMARY AND
IMPLICATIONS

11

SUMMARY, DISCUSSION, AND IMPLICATIONS

This book documents how two schools developed and implemented an elaborate teacher-as-youth-mentor system. This chapter summarizes the benefits of establishing such a system to students, teachers, and schools as a whole. It also lists some important principles to follow and barriers to overcome when attempting to implement such schemes. Finally, this chapter considers some implications for further research in the area of teacher-youth mentoring.

Benefits of Teacher-Youth Mentoring

Student Benefits

With the emphasis on high-stakes testing as mandated under No Child Left Behind, learning and academic success have been narrowly defined, and students have increasingly experienced a restricted and unnurturing environment (Barrier-Ferreira, 2008). Duffy, Giordano, Farrell, Paneque, and Crump (2008) elaborate on the impact of high-stakes testing, stating,

> Programs and services that allow students to explore topics related to the understanding and care of their physical and emotional health, the role of culture, the importance of family, and how to get along with others are likewise limited or reduced. (p. 11)

Further consequences of this restricted school environment and focus on testing are students' increased feelings of stress and anxiety (Kruger, Wandle, & Struzziero, 2007).

At both Fenway and Kedma, students and teachers indicated that the mentoring (called advisory at Fenway) systems created a space where both could relax and release anxieties. Students knew they had somewhere and someone to go to even if they were not doing well in academic classes. Furthermore, mentoring became a focal point for creating a community in the classroom. Students indicated that the experience in their mentoring classes enabled them to get to know their fellow students better, develop empathy with fellow students who were different from themselves, and gain new perspectives about their peers. Mentoring also helped solve peer conflicts and improved the overall classroom climate. Additionally, these systems ensured that students didn't fall between the cracks, but received full and personal attention. Students felt that there was a listening ear at the school and that teachers cared and were more responsive to their needs than teachers at other schools had been. Students found it very helpful to have mentors take on the role of advocates, mediating between them and other teachers; help them set high goals; help them find a balance among social life, work, and academics; and treat them as whole persons. Moreover, students felt that their abilities (and disabilities), culture, needs, and uniqueness were addressed and recognized. Because both teachers and students were recognized and attended to, neither party felt that there was a divide between the school and students.

The individual attention given to students and especially the extensive mental health support was instrumental for students with disabilities. Osher, Bear, Sprague, and Doyle (2010) concluded that programs attempting to meet the needs of students, such as Social and Emotional Learning programs and positive behavioral management, don't address students' mental health needs. Instead, they recommended creating more effective mental health services in schools by providing mental health support for teachers as well as for students.

Finally, although emotional and social support is important, the school's main role is to support students' academic achievement. As shown at Kedma and Fenway, mentoring supported not only the emotional and social needs of students, but also their academic needs by focusing on literacy skills, study skills, and the motivation to excel academically. Students were motivated to do well in school by being engaged academically, by displaying academic excellence through success on standardized tests, through achieving high graduation rates, and through using other measures of academic success. Addressing emotional and social aspects of students through mentoring classes, personal dialogues, and working with whole families was essential for students' academic success.

Teacher Benefits

Teachers at both schools expressed confidence in their own, as well as their colleagues', ability (collective efficacy) to connect with students and motivate them to succeed academically, and even persuade students to enroll in college. Given that most of the teachers have been mentoring and teaching students for a long time, and given that students had high social, emotional, and academic needs, this confidence was remarkable. Furthermore, these mentors displayed few signs of burnout or stress, as was evident by their continuous expression of commitment, love, and high expectations for their students. Goddard, LoGerfo, and Hoy (2004) recommend examining types of school reform that "build in teachers the resolve that they can effectively serve socioeconomically disadvantaged students" (p. 422). Indeed, both schools engaged in a long-term effort to create a student-centered environment through developing the advisory model that yielded the kind of school reform that enhances teachers' collective efficacy.

Several studies in the past decade have focused on the impact of collective teacher efficacy. These studies found that high collective teacher efficacy, as displayed at Fenway and Kedma, impacts student achievement more than students' socioeconomic status; helps students, especially poor and minority students, excel academically; and lowers teacher stress (Klassen, 2010). In discussing how schools might increase collective efficacy, Hoy, Sweetland, and Smith (2002) propose that schools invest in building teachers' capacity, as well as provide role models for teachers, verbal encouragement, and emotional support. Undoubtedly, both schools successfully met those recommendations. As for building capacity, teachers gained more control over the teaching process by interacting with their students both in academic and in mentoring classes. By getting to know their students academically, socially, and emotionally, teachers could effectively gear their curriculum and teaching methods to their students' needs. Peer support also enhanced mentors' capacity. The weekly meetings and support from mentor leaders, counselors, and psychologists allowed mentors to continuously assess and improve their capacity to better provide individual mentoring, advisory classes, and engage with parents. Furthermore, both schools provided ongoing professional development for mentors to help them better relate to students and create advisory activities that meet students' social, emotional, and academic needs.

Both schools also provided role models for advisors. The peer guides at Kedma and counselors at Fenway were excellent role models to the other mentors. The guides at Kedma were veteran mentors who modeled sensitive, thoughtful, and loving approaches to mentees. Counselors at Fenway, who had extensive background in addressing students' emotional and social needs, also served as advisors, and in turn as role models to their peers.

Finally, teachers found extensive verbal and emotional support at the schools. At Kedma, the mentors became the school's leadership team, and the principal continuously emphasized that they were the heart and soul of the school. The ongoing emotional support from weekly mentoring sessions, individual sessions with a psychologist, and close guidance from intervention psychologists were all key factors in the sustainability of Kedma's mentoring model. At Fenway, the house meetings and support by the house coordinator, the relaxed and supportive school environment, and retreats and events that allowed for informal and positive relationship building provided necessary advisor support.

In sum, mentors at both schools felt they were part of a community of educators who worked together to accomplish a common goal—nurturing and supporting urban minority students who often came from underserved communities.

School Benefits

School climate is crucial for reform to succeed. Both Kedma and Fenway emphasized establishing a fun and accepting environment, which created a foundation where youth mentoring thrived. The Race to the Top initiative is the most recent education reform passed by the United States government. This initiative calls for restructuring "failing" schools by, among other requirements, replacing principals and half of the staff and extending the school day—both of which are harsh and disruptive to staff and students. This initiative fails to address the most fundamental aspect of school reform—the school culture and environment. In analyzing the factors that promote sustainable school reform, Sergiovanni (2004) claims, "The answer is change forces that [are] based on [a] view of schools as communities" (p. 310). He further explains that school communities could emerge by focusing on three factors: relationships, place, and mind (or goals, values, and conceptions of being). Developing these aspects requires schools to nurture close connections among teachers, students, and parents; foster a shared sense of place; and work together to accomplish common goals and shared values. To promote school communities Sergiovanni (2004) poses important questions such as follows:

> What can be done to increase the sense of kinship, neighborliness, and collegiality among the faculty of schools? . . . What kinds of relationships need to be cultivated with parents that will enable them to be included? How can we redefine the web of relationships that exists among teachers and between teachers and students? How can teaching and learning settings be arranged so that they are more family-like? (p. 311)

Fenway and Kedma exemplify how school environment could be redefined to create a kinshiplike atmosphere where support for both teachers and students' social, emotional, and academic needs is relentless and long term.

Furthermore, both schools have been innovative by closely involving mental health professionals in the teaching and nurturing process. In a report about how to create schools that engage students, the National Research Council (2004) indicated,

> Current strategies to meet students' physical, social, and emotional needs are not accomplishing their purposes not only because they are underfunded and poorly organized . . . [but also] because students as learners cannot be divorced from students as people with social-emotional, physical, and mental health needs . . . [and therefore,] we recommend restructuring the roles of all school personnel, eliminating the notion that only counselors, social workers, and nurses are responsible for identifying and addressing students' nonacademic need. (p. 157)

Both schools undeniably provided models of how to break down the boundaries among teachers, guidance counselors, psychologists, and social workers. Advisors, most of who were teachers, school administrators, and other staff, assumed roles that were similar to guidance counselors as they engaged in advisory, individual mentoring, and communicating with families. Guidance counselors and psychologists also assumed new roles such as teaching (advisory classes) and mentoring teachers.

Another benefit of the mentoring models was school safety, for both schools had very little violence and teachers and students were often seen hugging and engaging in friendly conversations. When asked about discipline problems at Fenway, the security guard said that he had worked in many schools in Boston where he would break up fights and make arrests daily; however, at Fenway his main job was checking outsiders and securing the building. He added that students often came and introduced themselves to him and treated him as an ally rather than an adversary. Similarly, at Kedma the school environment felt safe and violence was rare. One fighting incident that was observed was stopped quickly and with little intervention. Similar to Fenway, security personnel at Kedma were usually used only to protect the school from outsiders. Indeed, research found that some of the most important elements that contributed to school safety were the focus on school bonding, supportive relationships between teachers and students, and close peer relations (Osher et al., 2010).

Implementation Principles

As the previous section indicates, the benefits of a well-planned teacher-as-youth-mentor program are enormous, but starting such a program can seem daunting. How should schools approach such a task and what guidelines should they follow? Furthermore, how could schools overcome barriers that stand in the way of a successful advisory implementation?

I. Guidelines for Establishing a Teacher-as-Youth-Mentoring System

Urban school reform needs to focus on the following seven guidelines:

1. Program creation through joint discourse and dialogue
    Kedma and Fenway created mentoring programs through dialogue and an ideology of commitment to promoting adult-student relationships. At Kedma, a grassroots organization engaged in a discourse about the gap between Mizrahi and Ashkenazi students. Out of this analysis, and based on the founders' own experiences in a discriminatory education system, they developed the principles that shape Kedma's philosophy and approach. At Fenway, the founders engaged in a dialogue with their students in what was an alternative program for disengaged students within the English High School of Boston. Through this discourse they developed a student-centered ideology that focused on listening to student needs and concerns. As a result

of this discourse, both schools developed nurturing metaphors (love and family) that reflected their ideologies. However, such student-centered emphasis could not be legislated through top-down processes. A key to long-term commitment to a student-centered school environment is the discourse process itself. Teachers, students, administrators, parents, and community members need to engage in a dialogue where everyone's voice is heard and the causes of dropout, violence, the achievement gap between privileged and underprivileged groups, and sources of inequality are honestly debated. It is through an honest discourse that a sustainable mentoring program would be possible.

2. Leadership with vision and commitment

Making a vision a reality in schools is difficult. Establishing a student-centered vision for schools does not guarantee implementation. Choosing leaders that commit themselves to the new ideology is crucial. The key to Kedma's and Fenway's success was leadership. The founding principals, Clara Yona-Meshumar, at Kedma, and Larry Myatt, at Fenway, as well as subsequent principals at both schools exemplified leadership with vision and commitment to providing a voice for students, staff, and parents. They also provided space for peers and colleagues to contribute to shaping the schools' future and vision. At Fenway, teachers and counselors engaged in developing and modifying the advisory that has evolved from a social issues class to its current format. At Kedma, mentors, under the leadership of mentor forum facilitator Bairy-Ben Ishay, were continuously challenged to develop their own voice and vision about mentoring and the school's philosophy. Therefore, it is essential that schools with intentions to create mentoring programs choose leaders who show long-term commitment to the endeavor.

3. Breaking down barriers

Schools are notorious for creating environments where teachers feel isolated, as the different units and roles within the schools are disconnected from one another. For example, schools have distinct roles for teachers and guidance staff based on division of labor—teachers focus on teaching academic skills, while mental health professionals focus on students' socialization, psychological problems, college applications, and scheduling. However, Kedma and Fenway created structures that reduced teacher isolation and provided opportunities for collaboration. Both schools created interdisciplinary courses, which were key to reducing segregation among discipline-based departments. Furthermore, mentors worked in pairs and engaged in weekly meetings with colleagues where they shared their concerns, tried new activities, and consulted colleagues. In addition, the roles of administrators, teachers, and counselors, especially in the case of Fenway, were often blurred, for all became mentors. Finally, the gap between parents and teachers was reduced so that parents and teachers became partners rather than adversaries. In short, a successful mentoring program reduces segregation among various stakeholders and structures within the school.

4. Staff development

Because teachers and administrators are often unprepared to deal with students' social and emotional issues, it is essential to create an ongoing staff development program. For example, at both schools mentors had frequent opportunities to try advisory activities on one another and conduct joint reflection. Mentors, counselors, and school psychologists often became resources for their colleagues in building their capacity as mentors; hence, it is essential that schools establish a plan for ongoing professional development for mentors to build their capacity to be nurturers and advocates for students.

5. Distributed leadership and participatory decision making

It was evident at both Kedma and Fenway that one of the major reasons for the sustainability of the mentoring program was the opportunities teachers and mentors had to provide leadership and participate in decision making. At Fenway, teachers and counselors were also house coordinators, leaders of after school programs, as well as professional development providers. As one school administrator intern at Fenway indicated, the school administrators rarely had to intervene in day-to-day teacher-student-parent issues because advisors were empowered to handle their own house issues and student problems. At Kedma, the mentor forum was the most important decision-making body at the school and determined important issues such as disciplinary decisions, academic calendar, and school events. Furthermore, veteran mentors often became guides to other mentors and attained leadership positions at the school, such as grade-level coordinators. Therefore, it is incumbent for schools to empower mentors so they will be more likely to have a long-term investment in their mentoring role.

6. Nurturing school environment

The mentoring program at both schools thrived due, in part, to establishing a nurturing school environment. Both schools created events and opportunities that promoted bonding among students and teachers, as well as ample opportunities to celebrate students' culture, identity, and accomplishments. This informal and friendly environment created a school climate where students wanted to be, and where they became more receptive to mentoring. Therefore, to create a successful mentoring program it is important to begin by creating a school climate that supports close relationships among members of the school.

7. Student-centered advisory curriculum

As indicated in chapter 3, advisories in secondary schools often do not have a consistent curriculum. Part two describes in detail the curricular elements essential to an advisory that meets the students' needs. One important principle is the emphasis on establishing a classroom community through activities that promote collaboration, self-disclosure, communication, close relationships, and dialogue. Another important aspect of a successful advisory program is promoting goal setting through self-reflection, career exploration, and planning for the future. A third component is helping students develop skills that facilitate academic success such as oral and written skills as well as study, organizational, time management, and test-anxiety reduction strategies. A fourth ingredient in a successful advisory program is addressing issues adolescents are most concerned with such as identity; family and personal relationships; gender and race; and health issues such as drugs, alcohol, and sex. For mentoring to reach students and address their needs, it is essential that an advisory program include these four elements. A sample list of mentoring class activities is described in the appendix.

II. Overcoming Barriers

Barriers to implementing successful teacher-as-youth-mentor programs are numerous. Potential impediments include the following: a crowded curriculum that emphasizes test preparation, leaving little space for a "soft" class like advisory; lack of financial resources to compensate mentors and additional expenses; school policies that discourage physical contact between teachers and students; large schools that make it difficult to create close relationships;

and lack of teacher preparation for mentoring roles. Below are some ideas and suggestions for overcoming these barriers.

1. Crowded curriculum

In an environment of standards-based curricula, secondary schools face a crowded course schedule that is filled with requirements. Creating interdisciplinary courses may ease the pressure of having to meet requirements for each discipline, reduce the crowded curriculum, and open space for an advisory class. For example, Fenway High School developed a humanities course that integrated social studies and English language arts, which freed up time in the schedule for an advisory class. Additionally, disciplines could be integrated into the advisory class. For example, the 10th grade advisory at Fenway integrated art into its curriculum enabling students to meet their art requirement within the advisory class.

2. Resource limitations

Educators and administrators often cite a lack of resources as a major impediment to education innovation. The mentoring programs at both schools required some additional resources. At Kedma, the school needed additional money to pay mentors for six hours per week for one-on-one teacher-youth mentoring, while at Fenway, additional resources were needed for teacher leadership and out-of-school activities. However, additional resources could be addressed in several ways. First, the small amount of money invested in the mentoring program could save much more in social services. Often, the separation between social services and schools results in the inefficient use of resources. The National Research Council (2004) indicated that services for students, especially low-income and minority students, tend to be rigid and disconnected where professionals who provide services to students know very little about their special needs and rarely develop close and trusting relationships with them. The council concluded, "The means to address students' nonacademic needs available in most high schools—career and academic counseling, mental health services, and a range of other problem-oriented services—are inadequate in amount and quality" (National Research Council, 2004, p. 156). Redesigning the teacher role as a mentor or an advisor enables student services to be much more efficiently coordinated. Indeed, at both Fenway and Kedma, mentors were often advocates and mediators for students not only among teachers but with outside agencies and social services such as probation officers and social workers as well.

Furthermore, restructuring the teacher's role to become one that supports students' social and emotional needs provides incentives for outside social agencies to form partnerships with these schools. In fact, as described in chapter 9, Kedma received free support in the form of psychologists and other professionals from two agencies because the agencies recognized the efficacy of the mentoring model in maximizing their ability to impact youth.

A second source of funding for a mentoring program could be found within the school itself. Most schools have resources allocated for coaches, department chairs, club advisors, team leaders, etc. By reexamining the school's priorities to focus on nurturing teacher-student relationships, the school could reallocate existing resources to establish and develop a viable advisory program. It was evident that focusing resources on mentoring enabled both schools to create a sustainable and affordable program. At Kedma, resources normally used for an on-site school counselor were reallocated to support the mentoring program and outside mental health support. At Fenway, eliminating an arts teaching position enabled the school to hire an additional counselor and provide more mental health support and professional development.

3. Policy barriers

School policies, often based on state and local school district guidelines, may impede school reform. Policies regarding limits on human contact between teachers and students could be a substantial barrier to an effective mentoring program. As described in this book, mentors at both Fenway and Kedma created close relationships with students that involved such physical contact as hugging and touching. Schools in the United States often consider physical touch between teachers and students taboo. In a qualitative study Andrzejewski and Davis (2008) found that four nurturing female teachers faced continual contradictions and dilemmas when making decisions regarding touching students. In addition, a survey of 515 New York State teachers found that fear of false allegations of sexual abuse, especially among male teachers at the high school level, had a chilling effect on teachers' willingness to hug or even put an arm around a student (Anderson & Levine 1999). The researchers recommended,

> Teachers and administrators may need to be more straightforward in their
> policies and in drawing lines between what is considered acceptable and

unacceptable behavior to avoid a chilling climate in which natural closeness is minimized to the student's detriment. (p. 842)

In other words, to establish an environment conducive to teacher-student mentoring programs, policy makers need to establish rules that facilitate trusting relationships between staff and students.

4. Large school size

A school should create a personalized and nurturing environment regardless of its size. While both Fenway and Kedma are small schools (300 and 150 students respectively), small size does not guarantee a nurturing environment. In a study comparing Kedma to a sister school of similar size and ideology, Ayalon (2004) found that the sister school failed to implement a viable teacher-as-youth-mentor program and its school climate was substantially less nurturing. Similarly, an ethnographic study of small schools in New York City found that small size did not always lead to close relationships between teachers and students (Shiller, 2009).

Conversely, a large school does not preclude its becoming a caring and personalized institution, but it might face additional challenges. Several studies of personalized school climate in large schools indicated that those large schools that achieved personalization had created mentoring programs for students. Chapter 3 describes a successful comprehensive school reform called First Things First (FTF) that included a family advocate system similar to the mentoring programs at Fenway and Kedma (Quint, Bloom, Rebek, Black, & Stephens 2005). The program was implemented in five school districts in Kansas, Mississippi, Missouri, and Texas with 22 middle and high schools, 13 of which had over 1,000 students and 1 school enrolled over 3,100 students. The FTF reform initiative also included creating small learning communities similar to the ones formed at Fenway High School. Another key ingredient of the reform was creating a forum for teachers to jointly work on instructional improvement—a feature regularly practiced at both Fenway and Kedma.

In another study of a large school, Bruenlin et al. (2005) describe an initiative to personalize a 3,700 student suburban high school. In addition to an advisory program, the school implemented five interventions: professional development for teachers on how to personalize their classrooms, a peer leadership program, conflict resolution training for students with violent discipline issues, a parent-community-school advisory group, and a teacher-administrator informal meeting team. Results indicated a significant improvement in the school climate.

In sum, it is more challenging to personalize large schools, but it is possible using principles similar to those implemented at Fenway and Kedma. It is essential that all schools establish structures that enhance cooperation and learning among students, adults, and parents, and where each school member is given individual attention and opportunities to interact informally, as well as to grow personally and academically.

5. Lack of teacher preparation

Teachers might argue that they are not counselors—they have enough to do. They don't have the knowledge to be youth mentors. As previously explained, a mentoring program has many teacher benefits, yet implementing such a reform is a demanding task. Research on Social and Emotional Learning (SEL), mentioned in chapter 2, is one source of information about appropriate professional development for mentors. Kress, Norris, Schoenholz, Elias, and Seigle (2004) found significant overlap between curriculum standards and SEL and suggested that training teachers in SEL strategies could contribute substantially to students' academic achievements.

Here are recommendations that schools could adopt in order to build teacher capacity to become youth mentors.

- **Teacher ownership**—Every school's administration and staff have to make sense of the mentoring program for themselves and be given time and resources to create their own structure and curriculum that addresses the social, emotional, and academic needs of its students and staff.
- **A developmental approach**—A school should continuously modify its mentoring program.
- **Whole-child metaphors**—Teachers should engage in discourse and adopt metaphors that promote the view of students as complex human beings who deserve nurturing and the view of themselves as educators who are able to help students. Teachers should be willing to listen, provide a safe space, engage in dialogue, and have high expectations for their students.

- **Learning to dialogue**—The school should teach and model for mentors how to conduct a dialogue with students that: provides positive feedback, identifies students' concerns, enhances students' self-understanding, shows care, creates connections with students, gets to know students' family situation, and remains focused on students' academic excellence.
- **Professional development**—Schools should welcome outside perspectives from such professionals as educators, mental health providers, and consultants who provide strategies and skills in enhancing teacher-student and teacher-teacher relationships. Furthermore, schools should encourage teachers to attend graduate-level programs that enhance their capacity to meet students' social, emotional, and academic needs, and promote a positive and nurturing school climate.

Research Implications

Schools are now increasingly incorporating advisory or teacher-as-youth-mentor programs into their curriculum. For example, anecdotal data of the Hartford, Connecticut, area schools indicated that at least seven middle and high schools are implementing such programs. However, the schools used a mixture of models that vary in number of weekly advisory meetings, amount of time allocated for each advisory, curriculum (and who plans it), and role of the mentors. For example, in one middle school the mentoring class meets every 10 days, with the mentors using predetermined and inflexible lesson plans, and their role does not incorporate parent communication. In another middle school, the mentoring class meets daily but some of the classes are dedicated to silent reading. Mentors prepare the advisory curriculum for other days, following a school-wide theme. Because mentoring programs vary, it is essential to conduct local and national surveys that document how often mentoring programs are used, their stated goals, and their effectiveness in reaching these goals. Furthermore, these research findings should be disseminated and benchmarked against the practice of effective mentoring models such as those described in this book, and used as a basis for analysis and exchange among researchers, educators, administrators, and policy makers.

The two case studies presented in this book raise many issues and challenges for further investigation. As previously indicated, schools routinely fail to implement advisory models in an effective and sustainable way. Research should be conducted on more schools in various settings to identify barriers to mentoring program implementation and ways to overcome them. Research also indicates that simply providing better instruction doesn't necessarily yield better student academic performance, for school climate is also influential. More specifically, close teacher-student relationships positively influence academic outcomes (Zullig, Koopman, Patton, & Ubbes, 2010). Therefore, it is recommended that school climate survey instruments be used to assess youth mentoring models. For example, surveys could indicate the degree to which mentoring programs increase school safety and decrease bullying behavior in schools.

Research could also explore whether advisory models enhance the efficacy of differentiated instruction. Because mentoring students promotes teachers' knowledge of students it could enable teachers to target instruction and curriculum to students' needs. Another important element is to investigate how mentoring programs are implemented in various countries. Cross-cultural studies, as exemplified by this book, could highlight how local conditions affect mentoring programs and the adjustments and modifications needed.

Another topic relevant to effective youth mentoring is the issue of shared decision making in schools. Because both Kedma and Fenway had high degrees of participatory decision making, it would be instructive to research the role shared decision making plays in the success of mentoring programs. Furthermore, given that both schools substantially incorporated mental health professionals, exploring effective advisory roles for counselors and school psychologists should be further researched. Research of school counselors' roles suggests that counselors are often assigned administrative roles that underutilize their professional skills, and are rarely given leadership roles. Janson, Stone, and Clark (2009) propose that counselors play an integral role in school leadership including such tasks as staff development, large group guidance, and college readiness and advising—roles that mental health professionals frequently assumed at Kedma and Fenway.

Parental views and roles in the mentoring model should also be explored. In this study, anecdotal data indicated that parents greatly benefited from, and supported, the mentoring model. However, more systematic research should be conducted to identify the most appropriate and effective ways to establish close connections between mentors and parents. Finally, in order to ensure successful mentoring programs, teachers and administrators need to be prepared for their role as nurturers. Teacher and administrator preparation programs should expand the curriculum to provide prospective teachers and administrators with strategies and dispositions that will enable them to better meet student needs. Topics such as conflict resolution, communication, study skills, and test anxiety should be incorporated into educator preparation programs. Research could focus on assessing the efficacy of such initiatives in promoting and enhancing mentoring programs and creating personalized schools.

List of Mentoring Activities

Note: games should include opportunities to process, reflect upon, and analyze what students learn from the games (such as, what did you learn today about yourself).

1. **Icebreakers/getting to know one another**

   True/False self-disclosure: Students make true and false statements about themselves. Peers have to guess what information is true and what is false.

   Getting to know you: Bring a personal item from home to share and explain why it is important.

   Appointment activity: Students use an appointment book to schedule a 5-minute appointment with each peer and use prepared questions to get to know one another. Students then share what they learned about their peers in class.

   Breakfast: Take student to breakfast or have students work together to prepare food together.

2. **Self-concept & peer support**

   Ping-pong: Students form a circle and throw a ball to one another. The student who throws the ball must say both something positive about the student he threw the ball to and something the student needs to improve on. Another version of this ball throwing exercise is to ask the student who catches the ball to express how he feels at school (assessing students' emotional status).

   Positive affirmation: Ask students to write their name at the top of a piece of paper. Pass the papers around the room and have each classmate write something positive on each paper.

3. Cooperative learning problem solving

Blindfolded pyramid building. Use cups to build a pyramid while being blindfolded. Allow the blindfolded student to use peer assistance, which will help the blindfolded student empathize with people who are visually impaired. The assisting peers learn how students handle stress and frustration.

Straw tower building: Teams compete within a time limit to see who can build the tallest tower from drinking straws and tape. Participants then analyze who emerged as leader or served other roles, what went wrong, what went right, who didn't say anything, etc.

Egg drop: Teams compete to see who can create a box that will prevent an egg from breaking on impact when the box is dropped from a certain height.

4. Goal setting

Wrapped box activity: Each student gets a wrapped box and lists what she/he would have liked to have in it or alternatively what she/he would like to put in it to get rid of.

Goal setting: Students choose among teacher-made written statements that describe future plans and each student explains orally to the class the reason for their choice.

5. Mapping students' emotional needs

Feeling cards: Distribute cards to students and ask them to complete sentences having to do with their feelings. For example, "When I am sad I feel . . ." The activity helps map the academic, social, and emotional needs of students.

Photo language: Hang a variety of pictures around the classroom that depict human relations or emotions. Ask students to pick pictures that are most meaningful to them and explain why they identify with them. Through this exercise students will learn about one another on a deeper level.

6. **Stereotypes/discrimination**

Social & personal awareness movies: Show a movie and afterwards conduct a classroom discussion asking students to make personal connections. Films could address parent-child relationships, day-to-day racial discrimination, gender attitudes among teenagers, sex education, weight, and social issues.

Gender issues: Ask students to fill out a gender stereotype survey or to list characteristics they are looking in a partner. Then divide students into single gender groups to discuss.

7. **Celebrating students**

Construct a class yearbook and celebrate students' heritage and culture (e.g. Latino month).

8. **Conflict resolution**

Role-play and self-analysis: Have students role play a common classroom behavior problem. Then ask students to analyze the incidents and make distinctions between thinking, feeling, saying, and doing.

9. **Discussions**

Circle up: This is a title given to class discussions during mentoring that follow a number of rules to ensure all students feel safe.

Current events: Discuss an important current event and connect it to students' personal lives.

10. **Values clarification**

Peer interview: Using teacher-made written questions, students conduct peer interviews in pairs taking turns as interviewers and interviewees about what they value and then share orally as a group. Questions could address such issues as the meaning of social justice, truth, friendship, etc.

11. **Organizational skills**

Create a student-made and decorated school calendar, or teach students how to organize their school bags.

12. **Critical thinking**—Use several principles to analyze issues/themes and self-behavior—PERCS

> Perspectives: Use theories (e.g Maslow's hierarchy of needs) or points of view (e.g teacher or peer) to analyze
>
> Evidence: Seek evidence to support the analysis
>
> Relevance: Find relevance to your own situation
>
> Connections: Make connections to other areas such as movies, stories, and events
>
> Suppositions: Examine your own beliefs as they connect to the issue at hand

13. **Interdisciplinary aspects**—You can incorporate most any discipline into an advisory activity. To incorporate language arts you could use poetry to discuss social relationships. Exercises that enhance students' written and oral communication skills are prevalent in advisory classes (such as the peanut butter sandwich exercise and peer critiques).

> Identity and self-expression through art and technology: Students create a representation of their face using Photoshop where half of the face includes objects that represent their identity and values.
>
> Poetry: Students discuss poems or sayings that address human relations such as the following saying: "Things that are given free are most dear, a simple hand, helping shoulder, sharing heart, nurturing soul. The most expensive things don't cost money but they [are] worth a fortune."

14. **Outside speakers**

> Both Kedma and Fenway used guest speakers in mentoring classes, especially in areas where advisors didn't have expertise or they felt someone else had more resources.

REFERENCES

Akos, P., Brown, D., & Galassi, J. P. (2004). School counselors' perceptions of the impact of high-stakes testing. *Professional School Counseling, 8*(1), 31–39.

Amos, J. (2008). *Dropouts, diplomas, and dollars: US high schools and the nation's economy.* Washington, DC: Alliance for Excellent Education.

Anderman, E. M. (2002). School effects on psychological outcomes during adolescence. *Journal of Educational Psychology, 94,* 795–809.

Anderson, A. R., Christenson, S. L., Sinclair, M. F., & Lehr, C. (2004). Check & connect: The importance of relationships for promoting engagement with school. *Journal of School Psychology, 42*(2), 95–113.

Anderson, E. M., & Levine, M. (1999). Concerns about allegations of child sexual abuse against teachers and the teaching environment. *Child Abuse & Neglect, 23*(8), 833–843.

Andrzejewski, C. E., & Davis, H. A. (2008). Human contact in the classroom: Exploring how teachers talk about and negotiate touching students. *Teaching and Teacher Education, 24,* 779–794.

Anfara, V. A. (2006). Advisor-advisee programs: Important but problematic. *Middle School Journal, 38*(1), 54–60.

Antrop-González, R. (2006). Toward the school as sanctuary concept in multicultural urban education: Implications for small high school reform. *Curriculum Inquiry, 36*(3), 273–301.

Ayalon, A. (2004). Successful grassroots school reform for marginalized groups—a case comparison. *Curriculum and Teaching, 19*(1), 83–103.

Ayalon, H., & Shavit, Y. (2004). Educational reforms and inequalities in Israel: The MMI hypothesis revisited. *Sociology of Education, 77*(2), 103–120.

Bairy-Ben Ishay, A. (1998). *Teacher burnout and consciousness-complexity—an analysis of the mentors at Kedma.* Dissertation Abstract, Harvard University.

Balfanz, R., & Legters, N. (2004). *Locating the dropout crisis: Which high schools produce the nation's dropouts?* Baltimore, MD: Johns Hopkins University Center for the Social Organization of Schools.

Barrier-Ferreira, J. (2008). Producing commodities or educating children: Nurturing the personal growth of students in the face of standardized testing. *Clearing House, 81*(3), 138–140.

Bar Shalom, Y. (2004). *The "Tikkun" idea: Educational entrepreneurship in Israel's multicultural society.* Tel Aviv, Israel: Kibbutz Hameuchad Publishing House.

Benard, B. (2004). *Resiliency: What we have learned.* San Francisco, CA: WestEd.

Bernstine-Yamashiro, B. (2004). Learning relationships: Teacher-student connections, learning, and identity in high school. *New Directions for Youth Development, 103*, 55–70.

Bogen, M. (2007). Getting advisory right. *Harvard Education, 23*(1), 4–6.

Borman, G. D., Hewes, G. M., Overman, L. T., & Brown, S. (2003). Comprehensive school reform and achievement: A meta-analysis. *Review of Educational Research, 73*(2), 125–230.

Boston Public Schools. (2009). *Introducing the Boston Public Schools 2009: A guide for parents and students.* Boston, MA: Author.

Brand, S., Felner, R. D., Seitsinger, A., Burns, A., & Bolton, N. (2008). A large-scale study of the assessment of the social environment of middle and secondary schools: The validity and utility of teachers' ratings of school climate, cultural pluralism, and safety problems for understanding school effects and school improvement. *Journal of School Psychology, 46*(5), 507–535.

Brendtro, L. K., Brokenleg, M., & Van Bockern, S. (2002). *Reclaiming youth at risk.* Bloomington, IN: Solution Tree.

Bridgeland, J. M., Dilulio, J. J., & Morison, K. B. (2006). *The silent epidemic: Perspectives of high school dropouts.* Civic Enterprises for Gates Foundation. Retrieved from www.gatesfoundation.org

Brown, J. H. (2004). Resilience: From program to process. *California Association of School Psychologists, 9*, 83–92.

Bruenlin, D. C., Mann, B. J., Kelly, D., Cimmarusti, R. A., Dunne, L., & Lieber, C. M. (2005). Personalizing a large comprehensive high school. *NASSP Bulletin, 89*(645), 24–42.

Chambliss, L. V. M. (2007). Creating classroom cultures: One teacher, two lessons, and a high-stakes test. *Anthropology & Education Quarterly, 38*(1), 57–75.

Christenson, S. L., & Havsy, L. H. (2004). Family-school-peer relationships: Significance for social, emotional, and academic learning. In J. E. Zins, R. P. Weissberg, M. C. Wang, & H. J. Walberg (Eds.), *Building academic success on social and emotional learning* (pp. 59–75). New York, NY: Teachers College Press.

Cleary, M., & English, G. (2005). The small schools movement: Implications for health education. *Journal of School Health, 75*(7), 243–247.

Comer, J. P., Haynes, N. M., Joyner, E. T., & Ben Avie, M. (1996). *Rallying the whole village: The comer process for reforming education.* New York, NY: Teachers College Press.

Committee on Increasing High School Students' Engagement and Motivation to Learn. (2004). *Engaging schools*. Washington, DC: The National Academies Press.

Conchas, G. Q., & Rodriguez, L. F. (2008). *Small schools and urban youth*. Thousand Oaks, CA: Corwin Press.

Crosnoe, R., Johnson, M. K., & Elder, G. H. (2004). Intergenerational bonding in school: The behavioral and contextual correlates of student-teacher relationships. *Sociology of Education, 77*, 60–81.

Dappen, L. D., & Isernhagen, J. C. (2005). Developing a student mentoring program: Building connections for at-risk students. *Preventing School Failure, 49*(3), 21–25.

Darling-Hammond, L. (1997). *The right to learn*. San Francisco, CA: Jossey-Bass.

DeSocio, J., VanCura, M., Nelson, L. A., Hewitt, G., Kitzman, H., & Cole, R. (2007). Engaging truant adolescents: Results from a multifaceted intervention pilot. *Preventing School Failure, 51*(3), 3–11.

DuBois, D., Holloway, B., Valentine, J., & Cooper, H. (2002). Effectiveness of mentoring for youth: A meta-analysis review. *American Journal of Community Psychology, 30*(2), 157–197.

Duffy, M., Giordano, V. A., Farrell, J. B., Paneque, O. M., & Crump, G. B. (2008). No Child Left Behind: Values and research issues in high-stakes assessments. *Counseling & Values, 53*(1), 53–66.

Editorial Projects in Education. (2008). Diplomas count 2008: Ready for what? Preparing students for college, careers, and life after high school. *Education Week, 26*(40), 40–41.

Ennis, C. D., & McCauley, M. T. (2002). Creating classroom communities worthy of trust. *Journal of Curriculum Studies, 34*(2), 149–172.

Everston, C. M., & Smithey, M. W. (2000). Mentoring effect on protégés' classroom practice: An experimental field study. *The Journal of Educational Research, 93*(5), 294–304.

Fenway Annual Report (2007/2008). *Fenway High School*. Boston, MA.

Fenway High School website. (2009a). http://www.fenwayhs.org/Background.htm

Fenway High School website. (2009b). http://www.fenwayhs.org/ventures.htm

Ferguson, R. F., & Snipes, J. (1994). Outcomes of mentoring: Healthy identities for youth. *Reclaiming Children and Youth, 3*(2), 19–22.

Finn, J. D. (1989). Withdrawing from school. *Review of Educational Research, 59*, 117–142.

Fredriksen, K., & Rhodes, J. (2004). The role of teacher relationships in the lives of students. *New Directions for Youth Development, 103*, 45–54.

Galassi, J. P., Gulledge, S. A., & Cox, N. D. (1997). Middle school advisories: Retrospect and prospect. *Review of Educational Research, 67*(3), 301–338.

Garibaldi, A. M. (1992). Educating and motivating African American males to succeed. *Journal of Negro Education, 61*(1), 4–11.

Gayler, K. (2005). *How have high school exit exams changed our schools? Some perspectives from Virginia and Maryland.* Washington, DC: Center on Educational Policy.

George, P. S., & Alexander, W. M. (2003). *The exemplary middle school* (3rd ed). Belmont, CA: Wadsworth.

Goddard, R. D., LoGerfo, L., & Hoy, W. K. (2004). High school accountability: The role of perceived collective efficacy. *Educational Policy, 18*(3), 403–425.

Grossman, J. B., & Rhodes, J. E. (2002). The test of time: Predictors and effects of duration in youth mentoring programs. *American Journal of Community Psychology, 30*(2), 199–219.

Haaretz. (2006, August 28). 50 most influential on education in Israel. *Haaretz Daily Newspaper*, special edition, 40.

Hackman, D. G. (2004). Constructivism and block scheduling: Making the connection. *Phi Delta Kappa, 85*, 697–702.

Hargreaves, A., & Fullan, M. (1998). *What's worth fighting for out there?* New York, NY: Teachers College Press.

Hargreaves, A., & Fullan, M. (2000). Mentoring in the new millennium. *Theory Into Practice, 39*(1), 50–56.

Haynes, N. M. (1996). Creating safe and caring school communities: Comer School Development Program schools. *Journal of Negro Education, 65*(3), 308–314.

Heale, W. H., & Scott, J. L. (2010). Making urban schools better places for students, teachers, and families: An interview with Charles Payne. *The Reading Teacher, 63*(8), 701–704.

Hickman, G. P., & Garvey, I. (2006). An analysis of academic achievement and school behavior problems as indices of program effectiveness among adolescents enrolled in a youth-based mentoring program. *Journal of At-Risk Issues, 12*(1), 1–9.

Hoy, W. K., Sweetland, S. R., & Smith, P. A. (2002). Toward an organizational model of achievement in high schools: The significance of collective efficacy. *Educational Administration Quarterly, 38*(1), 77–93.

Irvine, J. J. (1989). Beyond role models: An examination of cultural influences on the pedagogical perspectives of black teachers. *Peabody Journal of Education, 66*(4), 51–63.

Janson, C., Stone, C., & Clark, M. A. (2009). Stretching leadership: A distributed perspective for school counselor leaders. *Professional School Counseling, 13*(2), 98–106.

Jennings, J., Scott, C., & Kober, N. (2009). Rethinking "restructuring": Lessons learned from five states over five years. *Education Week, 28*(31), 36, 30.

Johnson, L. (2009). School contexts and student belonging: A mixed methods study of an innovative high school. *The School Community Journal, 19*(1), 99–118.

Kedma. (2009). *Dialog Hour: A book of activities* (first draft). Jerusalem, Israel: Kedma Publications. Retrieved from http://www.kedmaschool.org.il/main/siteNew/index.php?page=113&action=sidLink&stId=128.

Kedma Brochure. (1995). *Kedma for educational equality in Israel.* Tel Aviv, Israel: Kedma Association.

King, K. A., Vidourek, R. A., Davis, B., & McClellan, W. (2002). Increasing self-esteem and school connectedness through a multidimensional mentoring program. *Journal of School Health, 72*(7), 294–299.

Klassen, R. M. (2010). Teacher stress: The mediating role of collective efficacy beliefs. *The Journal of Educational Research, 103*, 342–350.

Kress, J. S., Norris, J. A., Schoenholz, D. A., Elias, M. J., & Seigle, P. (2004). Bringing together educational standards and social and emotional learning: Making the case for educators. *American Journal of Education, 111*(1), 68–89.

Krovetz, M. L. (1999). *Fostering resiliency.* Thousand Oaks, CA: Corwin Press.

Kruger, L. J., Wandle, C., & Struzziero, J. (2007). Coping with the stress of high stakes testing. *Journal of Applied School Psychology, 23*(2), 109–128.

Ladson-Billings, G. (1994). *The Dreamkeepers: Successful teachers of African American children.* San Francisco, CA: Jossey-Bass.

Landsman, J., & Lewis, C. W. (2006). *White teachers/diverse classrooms: A guide to building inclusive schools, promoting high expectations, and eliminating racism.* Sterling, VA: Stylus.

Lempers, J. D., & Clark-Lempers, D. S. (1992). Young, middle, and late adolescents' comparisons of the functional importance of five significant relationships. *Journal of Youth and Adolescence, 21*(1), 53–96.

Levin, H. M. (2009). The economic payoff to investing in educational justice. *Educational Researcher, 38*(1), 5–20.

Markovich, D. (2006). *Ethnicity, education and identity: The case of the Kedma academic community high school* (Dissertation abstract). Hebrew University, Jerusalem.

Moore, K. A., & Zaff, J. F. (2002). *Building a better teenager: A summary of what works in adolescent development.* Washington, DC: Child Trends.

Mor, F. (2003). *A study of psycho-educational intervention for effective educational work with underachieving youth at-risk in the education system* (Doctoral dissertation). University of Sussex, United Kingdom.

Murray, C. (2009). Parent and teacher relationships as predictors of school engagement and functioning among low-income urban youth. *Journal of Early Adolescence, 29*(3), 376–404.

National Association of Secondary School Principals. (2004). *Breakthrough high schools*. Reston, VA: Author.

National Research Council. (2004). *Engaging schools: Fostering high school students' motivation to learn*. Washington, DC: The National Academies Press.

Nelson, M., & Debacker, T. K. (2008). Achievement motivation in adolescents: The role of peer climate and best friends. *The Journal of Experimental Education, 76*(2), 170–189.

Newmann, F. M. (1981). Reducing student alienation in high schools: Implications of theory. *Harvard Education Review, 51*, 546–564.

Noam, G. G., & Fiore, N. (2004). Relationships across multiple settings: An overview. *New Directions for Youth Development, 103*, 9–16.

Noddings, N. (1984). *Caring: A feminine approach to ethics and moral education*. Berkeley, CA: University of California Press.

Noddings, N. (1992). *The challenge to care in schools: An alternative approach to education*. New York, NY: Teachers College Press.

Noddings, N. (2001). The caring teacher. In V. Richardson (Ed.), *Handbook of research on teaching* (pp. 99–105). Washington, DC: American Education Research Association.

Osher, D., Bear, G. G., Sprague, J. R., & Doyle, W. (2010). How can we improve school correction? *Educational Research, 39*(1), 48–58.

Osterman, K. F. (2000). Students' need for belonging in the school community. *Review of Educational Research, 70*, 323–367.

Oxley, D. (2007). *Small learning communities: Implementing and deepening practice*. Portland, OR: Northwest Regional Educational Laboratory.

Payne, A. A., Gottfredson, D. C., & Gottfredson, G. D. (2003). Schools as communities: Relationships among communal school organization, student bonding, and school disorder. *Criminology, 41*(3), 741–777.

Pianta, R. C., Stublman, M. W., & Hamre, B. K. (2002). How schools can do better: Fostering stronger connections between teachers and students. *New Directions for Youth Development, 93*, 91–107.

Prothrow-Stith, D., & Spivak, H. R. (2004). *Murder is no accident*. San Francisco, CA: Jossey-Bass.

Quint, J., Bloom, H. S., Rebek Black, A., & Stephens, I. (with Akey, T. M.). (2005). *The challenge of scaling up educational reform: Findings and lessons from First Things First*. New York, NY: Manpower Development Research Corporation.

Rallis, S. F. (1995). Creating learner-centered schools: Dreams and practice. *Theory Into Practice, 34*(4), 224–229.

Rhodes, J., Bogat, A., Roffman, J., Edelman, P., & Galasso, L. (2002). Youth mentoring in perspective: Introduction to the special issue. *American Journal of Community Psychology, 30*(2), 149–155.

Rhodes, J. E. (2001). *Stand by me: The risks and rewards of mentoring today's youth.* Cambridge, MA: Harvard University Press.

Rogers, C. R. (1980). *A way of being.* Boston: Houghton Mifflin.

Rockwell, S. (1997). Mentoring through accessible, authentic opportunities. *Preventing School Failure, 3*(41), 111–114.

Sanders, M. G. (1996). Action teams in action: Interviews and observations in three schools in the Baltimore School-Family-Community Partnership Program. *Journal of Education for Students Placed at Risk, 1*, 249–262.

Sergiovanni, T. J. (2004). Organization, market and community as strategies for change: What works best for deep changes in schools. In A. Hargreaves (Ed.), *Extending educational change* (pp. 291–315). New York, NY: Springer.

Sheleg, Y. (2005, February 4). Saving the world. *Haaretz Daily Newspaper*, 1.

Shiller, J. T. (2009). "These are our children!" An examination of relationship-building practices in urban high schools. *Urban Review: Issues and Ideas in Public Education, 41*(5), 461–485.

Sinclair, M. F., Christenson, S. L., & Thurlow, M. L. (2005). Promoting school completion of urban secondary youth with emotional or behavioral disabilities. *Exceptional Children, 71*(4), 465–482.

Sizer, T. R. (1984). *Horace's compromise: The dilemma of America's high schools.* Boston, MA: Houghton Mifflin.

Solomon, D., Battistich, V., Dong-il, K., & Watson, M. (1997). Teacher practices associated with students' sense of classroom as a community. *Social Psychology of Education, 1*, 235–267.

Spencer, R. (2004). Studying relationships in psychotherapy: An untapped resource for youth mentoring. *New Directions for Youth Development, 103*, 31–43.

Steinberg, I. (2002). *Adolescence.* New York, NY: McGraw-Hill.

Swaminathan, R. (2004). "It's my place": Student perspectives on urban school effectiveness. *School Effectiveness and School Improvement, 15*(1), 33–63.

Swirski, S., Konor-Atias, E., Kolovov, T., & Abu Hala, H. (2008). *Entitlement for Matriculation Exam by location: 2006–7.* Tel Aviv: Adva Center.

Vogler, K. E., & Virtue, D. (2007). "Just the facts, Ma'am": Teaching social studies in the era of standards and high-stakes testing. *The Social Studies, 98*(2), 54–58.

Walberg, H. J., Zins, J. E., & Weissberg, R. P. (2004). Recommendations and conclusions: Implications for practice, training, research, and policy. In J. E. Zins, R. P. Weissberg, M. C. Wang & H. J. Walberg (Eds.), *Building academic success on social and emotional learning* (pp. 209–217). New York, NY: Teachers College Press.

Watt, K. M., Powell, C. A., & Mendiola, I. D. (2004). Implications of one comprehensive school reform model for secondary school students underrepresented in higher education. *Journal of Education for Students Placed at Risk, 9*(3), 241–259.

Weinberger, E., & McCombs, B. L. (2003). Applying the LCPs to high school education. *Theory Into Practice, 42*(2), 117–126.

Wentzel, K. R., & Battle, A. A. (2001). Social relationships and school adjustment. In T. Urdan & F. Pajares (Eds.), *Adolescence and education: General issues in education.* Greenwich, CT: LAP Information Age Publishing.

Wilson, L., & Corbett, H. D. (2001). *Listening to urban kids.* Albany, NY: State University of New York Press.

Wimberly, G. (2002). *School relationships foster success for African American students.* Iowa City, IA: ACT Report. Retrieved from www.act.org

Woolley, M. E., & Bowen, G. L. (2007). In the context of risk: Supportive adults and the school engagement of middle school students. *Family Relations, 56*(1), 92–104.

Yona, I. (2002). *Voices from the Katamonim neighborhood.* Ramat Gan, Israel: Kedma Friends Association.

Zameret, Z. (1998). *Fifty years of education in the State of Israel.* Israel Ministry of Foreign Affairs. Retrieved from www.mfa.gov.il/mfa/go.as

Zins, J. E., Bloodworth, M. R., Weissberg, R. P., & Walberg, H. J. (2004). The scientific base linking social and emotional learning to school success. In J. E. Zins, R. P. Weissberg, M. C. Wang, & H. J. Walberg (Eds.), *Building academic success on social and emotional learning* (pp. 3–22). New York, NY: Teachers College Press.

Zullig, K. J., Koopman, T. M., Patton, J. M., & Ubbes, V. A. (2010). School climate: Historical review, instrument development, and school assessment. *Journal of Psychoeducational Assessment, 28*(2), 139–152.

INDEX

Also available from Stylus

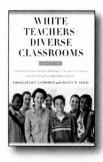

White Teachers / Diverse Classrooms
Creating Inclusive Schools, Building on Students' Diversity, and Providing True Educational Equity
Edited by Julie Landsman and Chance W. Lewis
SECOND EDITION

Acclaim for the first edition:

"Black and White teachers here provide an insightful approach to inclusive and equitable teaching and illustrate its transformative power to bring about success."—***Education Digest***

"Practical advice for teachers and administrators on ways to improve the education of students of color, emphasizing that low expectations are the worst form of racism."—***Education Week***

"This is a very good book for teachers to put on their shelves; I recommend its use at the university level as a teaching tool as well."—***Multicultural Review***

The point of departure for this new edition, as it was for the first, is the unacceptable reality that, for students of color, school is often not a place to learn but a place of low expectations and failure. In urban schools with concentrations of poverty, often fewer than half the ninth graders leave with a high school diploma.

This second edition has been considerably expanded with chapters that illuminate the Asian American, Native American, and Latina/o experience, including that of undocumented students, in our schools. These chapters offer insights into the concerns and issues students bring to the classroom. They also convey the importance for teachers, as they accept difference and develop cultural sensitivity, to see their students as individuals, and avoid generalizations.

Transforming Teacher Education
What Went Wrong with Teacher Training, and How We Can Fix It
Edited by Valerie Hill-Jackson and Chance W. Lewis
Foreword by Peter McLaren

Extracts from the text:

"Why are fifteen million children and youth in poverty not achieving when we know that low-income students excel in the classrooms of "star" teachers (who comprise approximately 8 percent of the teaching force)?"

"Whose needs or interests are being met in education reform today?"

"Why does teacher education focus on the managerial, instrumental or delivery system aspects of the profession?"

In this book, 12 distinguished scholars provide a hard-hitting, thoroughly researched, historical and theoretical critique of our schools of education, and offer clear recommendations on what must be done to ensure all children can achieve their potential, and contribute to a vibrant, democratic society.

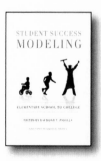

Student Success Modeling
Elementary School to College
Edited by Raymond V. Padilla
Foreword by Sarita E. Brown

"Focusing on the reasons for success in student performance rather than failure, Padilla (education and human development, U. of Texas at San Antonio) presents a framework for understanding student success and how it can be improved and replicated. He presents a general model and one for specific, local situations and how they have been applied in a minority high school, community college, and Hispanic-Serving University, and to compare high-performing and non- high-performing elementary schools. Chapters address the characteristics of students, teachers, and the school, its resources, and barriers to success."—***Book News Inc***

22883 Quicksilver Drive
Sterling, VA 20166-2102

Subscribe to our e-mail alerts: www.Styluspub.com